W9-ASG-168

Twayne's United States Authors Series

SYLVIA E. BOWMAN, *Editor*

INDIANA UNIVERSITY

J. F. Powers

J. F. POWERS

By JOHN V. HAGOPIAN
State University of New York at Binghamton

Twayne Publishers, Inc. :: New York

Library of Congress Catalog Card Number: 67-28860

MANUFACTURED IN THE UNITED STATES OF AMERICA BY
UNITED PRINTING SERVICES, INC.
NEW HAVEN, CONN.

For Susie
And for Amy and Geoffrey,
My Hostages to Fortune

Preface

ALTHOUGH he is a writer's writer, J. F. Powers has no broad popular following but is known among his peers as a brilliant satirist and meticulous craftsman. His fiction is widely anthologized and often taught in the universities; it may receive even wider attention now that *Morte D'Urban* is published by Modern Library. Although he has published only two volumes of short stories, a novel, a novella, and a small handful of uncollected pieces, Powers' first story appeared almost a quarter-century ago. He is now in mid-career. He works very slowly and carefully, and he has said that he will probably not publish more than two or three more novels. That limited production has made it possible for this study to be more than an introductory survey; it is an explication in depth.

I began this book with considerable trepidation. Among other things, I knew that to many it would seem presumptuous for a man who was not a Catholic to deal properly with fiction deeply rooted in Catholic values. But Powers himself assured me that a critic's lack of religious faith was not necessarily an obstacle, though he was very reluctant to have me or anyone else write a book about his work. During my visit to him in Greystone, Ireland, in 1964, and in subsequent correspondence, he was most cordial and cooperative. However, I would not want to give the impression that this study appears with his blessings. On the contrary, he has read and severely criticized the first rough draft. I have made extensive revisions, especially in my treatment of Powers' biography, and now present it with the genuine conviction that it is as fair and honest as I can make it.

I am grateful to the Research Foundation of the State University of New York for a grant-in-aid which made possible my trips to Ireland and throughout the Midwest for interviews with Charles Shattuck, Father George Garrelts, Richard Keefe, Sister Mariella Gable, O.S.B., and Mary Humphrey. Bishop James Shannon, Father Edgar Eberle, Father John J. Kirvan, Marie J. Hénault, Bergen Evans, and Martin Dolch have graciously corresponded with me about Powers' life and work. In Germany—

at the University of the Saar, the Falkenstein Seminar, and the Amerika-Haus Seminar in Kaiserslautern—and in the United States at Harpur College, I have learned a great deal from discussions with enthusiastic students. Besides J. F. Powers, several persons—Sister Mariella Gable, Charles Shattuck, Melvin Seiden, Sheldon Grebstein, Sylvia Horowitz, and Luise Cunliffe—have made valuable comments on the manuscript. David Levene assisted me in locating certain legal documents. Lesley Brill checked my quotations, and Martin Dolch and Louise Sohr proofread the text. My patient wife, Sue Hagopian, has been cooperative in every way. I owe her more than it is possible or appropriate to articulate here. To all these I offer my sincere thanks and impose no responsibility for my errors and shortcomings.

Doubleday & Co. has graciously given permission to quote from Powers' books and to reproduce the coat of arms on the title page of *Morte D'Urban*. Part of Chapter III has appeared in *Studies in Short Fiction* and Chapter IV, revised, in *Wisconsin Studies in Contemporary Literature*.

J. V. HAGOPIAN

State University of New York at Binghamton

Contents

Chronology

1917 James Farl Powers born July 8 in Jacksonville, Illinois, to James Ansbury and Zella Routzong Powers.

1924 Family moved to Rockford, Illinois, where Powers attended public school.

1931 Family moved to St. Peter's parish in Quincy, Illinois; Powers attended Quincy Academy, taught by Franciscan Fathers.

1935 Graduated; went to live with family and sought employment in Chicago.

1936 Salesman for Fidelity Insurance Company at $15 per week; then sales clerk at Marshall Field & Co.

1936-1937 Chauffeured wealthy investor through the South.

1938-1941 Editor with Chicago Historical Records Survey at $80 per month; attended night classes at Northwestern University.

1942 Clerk at Brentano's bookstore; wrote first short story, "He Don't Plant Cotton."

1943 Experienced religious crisis and made one-man retreat in Oakmont, Pennsylvania; became pacifist.

1944 Employed as hospital orderly in St. Paul, Minnesota; "Lions, Harts, Leaping Does" included in O. Henry and Martha Foley anthologies.

1946 Married Betty Wahl and lived in Avon, Minnesota.

1947 Resident at Yaddo; published *Prince of Darkness.*

1948 Taught at St. John's College, Minnesota; received grants from Guggenheim Foundation and the National Institute of Arts and Letters.

1949-1951 Taught at Marquette University in Milwaukee. Resident at Yaddo.

1951-1952 Lived in Greystones, County Wicklow, Ireland.

1952-1956 Lived in St. Cloud, Minnesota.

1956 Published *The Presence of Grace;* taught at University of Michigan.

1957-1958 Lived in Dalkey, County Dublin, Ireland.

1958-1963 Lived in St. Cloud, Minnesota.

1962 Published *Morte D'Urban,* which won National Book Award.

1963-1965 Lived in Greystones, County Wicklow, Ireland; worked on *Bill and Joe.*

1965 Writer-in-residence, Smith College, Northampton, Massachusetts.

J. F. Powers

CHAPTER 1

The Man and His Values

READERS familiar with one or two of J. F. Powers' widely anthologized stories, such as "The Valiant Woman" and "The Forks," generally regard him as an interesting but parochial figure—a specialist in priests. Much of his Catholic audience, uneasy with Powers' scorn for sentimental piety, enjoy his writing as a kind of family joke that would best not be shared with outsiders. His taut, understated ironies are out of step with current literary fashions, and he avoids lecture circuits and cocktail parties. As a consequence, Powers remains on the periphery of the literary stage, even though he is, as Frank O'Connor says, "among the greatest of living story-tellers."[1] Out of parochial materials he shapes subtle but highly charged human situations that capture the moral and emotional texture of modern life. And he does so with such immense skill and tough-minded compassion that his writing will surely endure.

I *Literary Influences and Credo*

A prelude to the study of J. F. Powers' fiction might well be an account of his conception of the techniques and purposes of his writing and of the influences that have helped to shape them.[2] Although he has never made a formal statement of his literary esthetics, everything that Powers has recorded in print on such matters indicates that he has a clear and consistent literary philosophy. Apparent contradictions in his understanding of his own work disappear when they are placed in a proper perspective. For example, upon receiving the National Book Award for *Morte D'Urban*, he declared: "Philosophically, I'm a Catholic Writer. . . . I'm a writer who got into this thing and did it a little better than anyone else had done it. This country is decidedly a specialist's country and I think it's happening to me.

I know that sounds like I'm a gall-bladder man, but it does happen."[3] But a year later, when asked if he had "any ideas about the special vocation of the Catholic writer," he replied: "No, . . . except that obviously he should not write junk." He then expressed considerable annoyance about the reception of *Morte D'Urban* in certain places: "It was presented as a book about priests, about Catholics for Catholics. . . . Would you say that *The Wind in the Willows* is a book for animals?"[4]

This is an old problem faced by many writers whose identities, affiliations, or subject-matter in any way departs from cultural norms. Recently Rajo Rao, author of *Kanthapura* and *The Cat and Shakespeare*, felt compelled to declare that he is "not an Indian writer. 'I'm a writer,' he said, 'whose subject is contemporary life in India and whose background is in India, but I should not be considered an Indian writer and my books should not be reviewed by specialists on India but simply by good judges of literature.' "[5] Similarly, James Baldwin once explained that he left America because "I wanted to prevent myself from becoming *merely* a Negro, or even merely a Negro writer. I wanted to find out in what way the *specialness* of my experience could be made to connect me with other people instead of dividing me from them."[6]

But, if one *is* a Catholic, or an Indian, or a Negro, and if one writes out of the experiences and values he has most intimately lived, he cannot so simply deny his obvious identity. In frustration Baldwin was—like Powers—forced to concede and again to qualify: "I am an artist. . . . And let's face it, I'm a *Negro* artist. . . . [but] I get so tired of black and white. . . . I'm trying to find another word besides Negro to say what I mean."[7] Powers, too, has faced this dilemma. Asked if he thought the terms "Catholic literature" and "Catholic fiction" were meaningful, he replied, "I think they are meaningful, but I do not like them. . . . To say Mauriac is a Catholic writer, or Graham Greene is a Catholic writer—I suppose that's true; but, more than that, they are writers."[8]

Thus, as a writer, Powers tries to place his artistry above and even in opposition to his religion: "There is a necessary contradiction between the artist and the saint, a question of ends even more than of means, and those two shall never meet; though, when there is a little of both in a man, you might sometimes think so."[9] On another occasion Powers reiterated this contradiction: "Mr. Greene claims that he, as a writer, must be 'disloyal' to his religion. I assume this to be his way of calling attention to the inexorable demands made upon him or any serious writer by literature, demands that keep him from becoming the saint that his religion assures him it is within his power to become, and his duty. It is a nice dilemma, perhaps best resolved, or cushioned, by marriage with a good woman and the ensuing necessity to abstain from either course."[10]

Apparently then, although Powers believes that at times priests can be artists—at least in their sermons—there is no requirement that the artist, even the Catholic artist, be a priest.[11] This attitude distresses more than one of the clerical critics of Powers' work, who would love nothing more than to claim one of the most important of modern American writers as their own—but wish to do so only on their own terms. For example, Sister M. Bernetta Quinn, O.S.F., balances and re-balances the scales until she is almost forced to throw up her hands in frustration before arriving at a judicious, accurate final estimate: "Unambiguously the term *Catholic* before physician, teacher, butcher, engineer, refers to the fact that each of these persons belongs to the Catholic Church. Yet if the adjective *Catholic* is prefixed to *writer* ambiguity immediately results. Does the speaker mean someone who, whether a Catholic or not, presents a view of reality similar to or identical with that held by those within the Church, or a writer who happens to be a Catholic and who may or may not let this commitment be evident in what he writes?"

Taking a cue from Flannery O'Connor, who—unlike Powers—never found that belief in Christian dogma is a hindrance to a writer, Sister Bernetta makes an untenable generalization: "The Catholic writer reveals reality: all writers, to the extent they do this, are Catholic writers." By such a criterion Powers appears less Catholic than Miss O'Connor because he does not see reality as deeply as she does: "The satirist heightens reality; moreover, he is concerned with surfaces, not depths." Yet Sister Bernetta proceeds to argue that J. F. Powers is a Catholic writer in spite of his professed Joycean spirit, and she rebukes another critic, Robert Bowen, for asserting that "J. F. Powers is best thought of not as a Catholic writer but as a writer who happens to be Catholic."

Sister Bernetta apparently believes that Powers has no choice over a matter which is providentially arranged: "No person who is faithful to his native endowments 'happens' to be what he is; his role in the Mystical Body (and the 'presence of grace' entitles Powers to inclusion in this) is providentially arranged. . . . Powers writes of everyday incidents which when cumulated achieve as great a horror as the more violent subjects of the Southern story-teller, *because they represent treason to an ideal.*"[12] Whether Providence has arranged for J. F. Powers' role in the Mystical Body or not is a question outside the province of literary criticism, but it is certainly true that an ideal which may be described as Catholic, and occasional treason to it, are manifested in his fiction.

However, Sister Bernetta fails to make the necessary distinction between Powers' deep faith in a permanent religious ideal and his criticism of a constantly changing temporal institution, the Roman Catholic Church, of which Powers has said, "there's nothing bigger, cruder, more vulgar in the world."[13] It is, in fact, his high conception of the ideal that makes him so trenchant a satirist of the institution. On the other hand, it is not quite accurate to say that "J. F. Powers, an ardent and militant Catholic, has practically devoted his life to an attempt to keep unfit priests out of the Church."[14] His primary role is that of artist, not that of reformer or propagandist.

By no means a "devout" Catholic—"I hate that word applied to me"[15]—Powers is meticulous about attending mass regularly and going to confession at least once a year, but he doesn't always enjoy the experience:

> Going to church . . . can be a source of much woe. I myself have suffered all my adult life from something I can only describe as My Sunday Sickness. This is what comes from listening intently during the sermon. Sleepers and the indifferent Awake are never afflicted . . . They are there, as they should be, for the Mass, and in that circumstance is one of the differences between Catholic and Protestant and also the reason our sermons on the whole are no better than they need be. [At a church sermon] recently I was advised to go to the attic few of us have any more and find my old catechism—ten readings a day would dispel the darkness, a really charitable diagnosis of my needs, but one for which I could be, only in a way, grateful.[16]

The frequent failure of the Church to live up to its own lofty vision or to face the moral complexities of contemporary life arouses Powers' satirical ire—which, in turn, often arouses the ire of his clerical targets. Yet Powers remains confident of his fundamental orthodoxy: "they may think I'm a damned nuisance," he says, "but I'm not heretical."[17] Though he believes that a writer must separate his obligations to his craft and to his Church, he scorns the notion that the writer must therefore eschew all spiritual commitments: "I would not fly blind and write without regard to a body of philosophy. . . . There are laws, moral laws, as real as gravity." However, he does not seek to convert his readers to those laws:

> I would hope that [in some reader somewhere, some change might come about if he discovers himself in one of my stories], if I thought it were hopeable, but I do not. I don't even think of that, not once, when I write a story. I mostly think about giving somebody an experience. I'm a performer in that sense. I'm a little monkey with a cup. . . .
>
> . . . Art is a kind of magic. It can perform miracles when it is working—in you when you are writing, and later in the reader. There are people who are absolutely oblivious of this element. . . .
>
> . . . Somewhere along the line something has to happen. Grace has to take over. It can happen in as many different ways as there are people. There are things you should do and can do, but you cannot teach sanctity, can you?[18]

In mastering the art of rendering experience, Powers has had the help of trained and sympathetic critics. He candidly acknowledges that as a student he "was helped by a teacher who has since become famous, Bergen Evans at Northwestern. He told me where I was bad, where I was callow—and I was callow all over the place. I had the feeling that he knew what he was talking about. I did not have the feeling that he was somebody being polite, somebody being decent, somebody sending away a defender of his reputation."[19] And Powers has often acknowledged the help he has received from the editors of the various journals in which he has published—especially to Charles Shattuck of *Accent,* where he published the first stories that attracted serious attention. Shattuck provided "invaluable criticism when it was hard to get anyone to look at my work."[20] Powers has appropriately dedicated his first book, *Prince of Darkness,* "to Chuck and Kerker in gratitude" (the latter being Kerker Quinn, co-editor of *Accent* in the 1940's).

A more recent influence has been that of the editors of the *New Yorker,* first Katherine White (the wife of E. B. White) and most recently Robert Henderson.[21] Nine of Powers' stories, including four chapters from *Morte D'Urban,* were first published there. When asked if the editors had ever been responsible for significant changes in his work, Powers replied: "Well, they have their objections, but they haven't tampered with my stuff. I don't mean it's published as I first wrote it. Very often they have an objection to this or that aspect of it, or they want me to clarify it, and I will. It always gets better, improves with re-writing. When I put a book of stories together, I don't worry about the *New Yorker* stories at all. I know they make sense and are grammatical and that they are clear, as clear as I can be. . . ."[22]

Even more important has been the influence and example of other writers, especially Evelyn Waugh and Katherine Anne Porter.[23] These two form, no doubt, a curious combination of influences, Waugh being one of the most prolific and devastating satirists of the century, and Miss Porter a sparing and meticulous literary artist. Powers says of Evelyn Waugh, "I could re-read any of his books tonight. I don't feel that way about any other writer. . . . The writing can be very simple, but it holds on in a kind of funny way. It doesn't sweat, though sweating was involved, and it doesn't miss. It doesn't seem to care, to try very hard. It's just devastating."[24]

And of Katherine Anne Porter, whom he considers "first among American writers," he says: "She hasn't written any 'yarns,' and she hasn't let the demons take over. She has approached life reverently in her stories, and it lives on in them. . . . I think Katherine Anne Porter has usually worked on a higher wire than others: she has seen and felt more above *and* below, and, without huffing and puffing, has given us more—the nearest thing yet to reality in American fiction."[25]

Most of the other writers whom he has cited as important to him are also either comic satirists or meticulous craftsmen. The first group includes Sinclair Lewis ("the first serious writer I read, when I was about nineteen"), Aldous Huxley, Anthony

Trollope, Max Beerbohm, and Ring Lardner. Most important of the literary craftsmen is James Joyce ("who had a profound influence on me—*Ulysses*, a great book").[26] Others are F. Scott Fitzgerald, especially for *The Great Gatsby* ("Fitzgerald's best had always been the best there was")[27]; and Sherwood Anderson ("'I Want to Know Why' is a perfect short story: action and emotion suspended in counterpoise, and no ruminating detours").[28]

Being a writer whose prose is lean and severely controlled, Powers is simply unable to appreciate the more elaborate style of a writer like Faulkner. "With most novels that I read, I am just bored stiff. But I have been thinking that I ought to do more long, tiresome passages which would serve the purpose of making the good parts sound even better. I think that is the Faulkner technique. He didn't do it deliberately, but that is how it works out."[29] Similarly, but with somewhat more modesty, he finds Herman Melville outside his range of sympathy: "I don't run off at the mouth quite enough. The way the sea looked, or how the trolley came down the hill . . . the Melville kind of thing, where you give the history of whaling in a novel, or if you're a modern you give the history of sexual intercourse. I just don't do that. I'm impatient. I can't even read many of the great novels—so how can I begin to write them?"[30]

At the very beginning of his career, Powers wrote in a white heat of rage and indignation: "It was mostly anger. Anger at not being able to get a job; anger at the plight of the Negro; anger at other things I was just beginning to see."[31] But he has gradually mellowed and, though never a prolific writer, slowed down to one or two stories or chapters a year. He describes his pace with a Hemingway idiom: "I'm like a seasoned fighter, not a sucker for an easy punch; I can't write a lot of junk."[32] "I'm not going to be one of those writers who turn out a lot of books, and suddenly people wish they weren't being published."[33]

Powers keeps not only his pace but also his range within the limits most congenial to him. In this respect, he resembles Evelyn Waugh, of whom he has said: "Waugh does not attempt the impossible to him, to his method, and so he is never caught trying too hard, the common fault of satirists. He realizes he can turn so much lead into gold, quicksilver rather. It is silly to compare him . . . with humorists or with 'great' novelists. It would also be silly for Catholics to look to him for the kind of books already written by Bernanos and Greene and others. He does not seem to have the heart for that, nor, what is more discernable, the desire."[34] Like Waugh, Powers avoids the Gothic melodramatic effects of Bernanos and Greene; and, again like Waugh, Powers is "a man with an infinite possibility of creative irritation when observing the behaviour of his fellow men."[35]

Nevertheless, Powers cannot be described as "Waughspish," as *Time* puts it;[36] for Waugh's world is not made up "of consistent adult moral standards, since whatever justice there is is seldom tempered by compassion."[37] Some of Powers' fiction—a story like "Prince of Darkness"—might be described as "Waughspish" in tone; but, by and large, his irony is much more benign. A. E. Dyson has observed that there are at least three distinct uses of irony in satire: Jonathan Swift's destructive irony used as a weapon against certain evils; a more benign irony like that of Gibbon, which stresses positive values at the expense of forces that are undermining them; and a cynical irony like that of Evelyn Waugh, which lampoons gross evils and stupidities without clearly implying support of some opposing positive set of values.[38] Powers fits into the second rather than the third of Dyson's categories.

Then, too, there is a difference between the comic and the grotesque. Waugh is a ringmaster who cracks his whip and forces his creatures to go through their amusing but unnatural gestures. In Powers, the ironies are intrinsic to the natural behavior of his characters—natural, but comic by reference to an implicit Christian ideal. As he said to Sister Kristin:

> I see the human situation as essentially comic. . . . Here we are Christians, and here we have the clergy, who are descended spiritually from the apostles. Yet you know how we have to live if we are not to be certified as nuts. You are pastor of a big parish with people making money in (from the viewpoint of the Middle Ages, or even one hundred years ago) very odd ways. They do not do anything with their heads. They do not do anything with their hands. These are your parishioners. They have children, and you have to have a school, and schools cost money, and you have to have a bus, you have to have heat. You have to get some sisters to come in from somewhere, and they have to have a place

to live and all that. Well, you're a long way from Tipperary, to say nothing of Jerusalem, and anyone who begins to act like an apostle is subject to doubt, and rightly so, because the situation is so different. That's the irony of it.[39]

Many critics, like the Reverend James P. Shannon, have suspected that "possibly Powers' talent, like that of Evelyn Waugh, is that caustic kind which can only suggest the perfection of the ideal by its cutting exposition of the imperfect."[40] If so, Powers' life experiences are the acids which have tempered his Catholicism to the fine steel instrument it is today.

II *The Life*

James Farl Powers, a "cradle Catholic" and one of the three children of James Ansbury and Zella Routzong Powers, was born July 8, 1917, in Jacksonville, Illinois. Since his father was dairy-and-poultry manager for Swift & Company, the family was economically comfortable; and Powers grew up "the real American boy, playing baseball, basketball, and football"[41] in an atmosphere of bourgeois culture. His mother was an amateur painter and his father had been a child prodigy of the piano.[42] The autobiographical story, "Jamesie," evokes some of the experiences of his boyhood—selling *Liberty* magazine and Rosebud salve; reading Tom Swift, Horatio Alger, Jr., and *Sporting News*, as well as the Greek myths, the Arthurian legends, *Oliver Twist*, *Pinocchio*, and *Gulliver*.

Yet, as Powers himself has said, living in an area which was culturally a part of the South wasn't entirely pleasant: "The town was Protestant. The best people were Protestants and you felt that. That to some extent made a philosopher out of me. It made me mad."[43] Harvey Roche, the protagonist of *Morte D'Urban*, grew up in a town very much like Jacksonville, Illinois, where "Protestants were very sure of themselves. . . . If you were a Catholic boy . . . you felt that it was their country, handed down to them by the Pilgrims, George Washington, and others, and that they were taking a risk in letting you live in it."[44]

As a student at Quincy Academy in Illinois, Powers maintained an indifferent academic record; but he was proficient at athletics, especially basketball. His closest friends and teammates were

Elmo McClain (now coach and teacher at Christian Brothers High School in Quincy), Richard Keefe (now Dean of Admissions at St. Louis University), and George Garrelts (now priest in charge of the Newman Foundation at the University of Minnesota).

One of his teachers, Father Edgar Eberle, recalls:

> Jim and his pals were a likeable group, who not only enjoyed their athletics, but liked a lot of fun and nonsense. They were a noisy bunch. McClain, Keefe, and Garrelts could keep a group entertained on a trip with their tall stories, boasting, and make-believe. Jim was somewhat of a contrast with the other three, would listen a bit, and then set any of them down with some wry wit or sarcasm. I think it was a very fortunate thing for Jim to have such fine companionship. He was inclined to become moody and discouraged. It was the time of the depression and the gloomy outlook that young men had for their future in those days seemed to me to affect Jim more than the others.[45]

After graduation, Keefe and Garrelts entered the seminary, but Powers himself never considered becoming a priest: "I just didn't care for the look of the life. The praying would have attracted me. I wouldn't have minded the celibacy, but I wouldn't have liked the social side, the constant footwork. I couldn't see myself standing outside church Sunday morning talking to a bunch of old women."[46] He admits that "that doesn't say much for my understanding of the priesthood. On the other hand, there's an awful lot of *that*—all those young pastors in the suburbs who have to knock down thousands and thousands of dollars in order to build this and that. Well, what does that mean? Shaking hands with some guy, and you can't really tell him what's wrong with him, because he's got what you need."[47]

In 1935, Powers went to live with his parents and sought employment in Chicago. "It was a bad time for it. I worked in Marshall Field's department store, selling books, shirts, and even linoleum for a day. By 1936 there was not so much of the American boy in me, I think."[48] "This was the depression, and you can't remember what it was like. I was a miserable failure at getting a decent job; you could promise them anything—that you'd work extra hours in the morning and evening, that you wouldn't eat lunch—but it didn't matter. There was always someone willing to give them more."[49] In frustration, Powers took to spending his days in the reading room of the Chicago Public Library. When he did get a job as a salesman with the Fidelity Insurance Company, he found that he was temperamentally unsuited for the work. One of his satiric sketches cites a character named Jim, a "hard case" who "spent ten and fifteen minutes parked out in front of an account, afraid to go in, afraid he wouldn't be able to sell."[50]

In 1937, Powers became chauffeur to a wealthy investor and drove him in a new Packard through the South on a search for profitable investments. "I took my typewriter with me," Powers recalls. "I had some kind of idea that I needed it in my business—the only catch being: what was my business? I know now that I was a writer then, for better or worse. It was the only thing I cared about being."[51] In the following year he became an editor with the Chicago Historical Records Survey at eighty dollars a month and enrolled in night classes at the Chicago branch of Northwestern University. When the survey was completed in 1941, Powers once again found himself unemployed and could not continue his education. He then got a job as a clerk in Brentano's bookshop, but after a year was dismissed for refusing to buy war bonds.

The Chicago of the early war years was a world unlike anything he had ever known. He was thrown into the company of a variety of social rebels—the Catholic Workers, Negro jazz musicians, political exiles from Europe, who became subjects for his stories when he began to write for publication. During this time the conflict between Powers' religious ideals and the demands of the secular world reached crisis proportions. Appalled by the wholesale slaughter and destruction of the war and revolted by the gaudy cheapness of jingoist propaganda, he became a pacifist.

Early in 1943, he attended a priests' retreat—the only layman there—conducted by Father John J. Hugo at St. John's Abbey in Collegeville, Minnesota. Father Hugo was, according to Father George Garrelts, a "priest from Pittsburgh who was preaching rather strong doctrine . . . about War and Pacifism and its relation to Christian life. It was a bold venture, but was the forerunner of the type of meeting that now goes on in many places—institutes for priests of various kinds. This was an institute on the spiritual life."[52] And Father Hugo reports that "naturally he heard a good deal, both about the ideals and the abuses of the clergy."[53]

Also in 1943 Powers conducted a one-man retreat at an orphanage in Oakmont, near Pittsburgh, where he did a great deal of intense reading in such books as Abbé Longpré's *Le Chrétien en Retraite* and "lived under the ether of deeply-felt convictions."[54] He emerged from this experience to write his first mature story, the tenderly elegiac "Lions, Harts, Leaping Does," about a dying priest who clings to his faith despite an overwhelming sense of his unworthiness. In that same year he published in *The Catholic Worker* three sketches which forcefully express his religious convictions at the age of twenty-five. He laments the fact that for most men "the upholstery of Christianity has held up better than the idea and practice,"[55] and he asserts that "a saint is not an abnormal person. He is simply a mature Christian. Anyone who is not a saint is spiritually undersized—the world is full of spiritual midgets."[56]

After refusing to serve in World War II, Powers went to work as an orderly in a Chicago hospital and continued to write stories. In 1945, he visited his friend Don Humphrey at the College of St. Benedict in St. Joseph, Minnesota, to commission a chalice and other altar pieces with the proceeds from his story, "Blessing." There he met Sister Mariella Gable, O.S.B., who had admired "Lions, Harts, Leaping Does" as a work of genius and had reprinted it in a collection entitled *Our Father's House* (1945). Sister Mariella persuaded him to read the manuscript of a novel by Elizabeth Alice Wahl, a shy and deeply religious student at St. Benedict's. J. F. Powers and Betty Wahl met on November 10, 1945; and in just two days they became engaged. Five months later they were married. One wedding photograph shows in attendance: Emerson Hynes (now special assistant to Senator Eugene McCarthy), Harry Sylvester (novelist), the late Don Humphrey (the artist), Father George Garrelts (now director of the Newman Foundation at the University of Minnesota), and John C. Haskins (poet and radio personality in Washington, D.C.).

During the first years of their marriage, Powers' income was limited to his salary from part-time teaching at St. John's College and to fellowships from the Guggenheim Foundation and the

National Institute of Arts and Letters. He and Betty lived in Avon, Minnesota, in the cellar of an unfinished house which he has called a "sunken grave"; but he asserts that "We were really happy then. We thought life was a thing for grasshoppers, a beer party, but it hasn't turned out that way."[57] For a brief period in 1947 Powers went to live at Yaddo to finish his first book, *Prince of Darkness*. The critical success of that book, as well as O. Henry citations for "Prince of Darkness" in 1946 and "The Valiant Woman" in 1947, made it possible for him to begin to appear in the better-paying, high-circulation periodicals such as *Collier's*, *New Yorker*, *Partisan Review*, and *The Reporter*; but his slow deliberate pace rarely permitted him to complete more than one story in a year.

His wife, too, began to publish in the *New Yorker* in 1947, but the ever-increasing demands of domesticity and child-rearing have unfortunately limited her production to about half a dozen stories. She has a marvelously deft, satiric touch of her own. "Martinmas," for example, is a witty depiction of the frustration of girls in a parochial school who are eager to learn about life, but who get from Father Gabrowski only a ridiculous allegorical parallel between abstract virtues and the parts of an automobile—and from Sister Genevieve the explanation that a French kiss is the effusive touching of cheeks by French generals.[58]

Another of her stories, "Gingerbread," is a tautly controlled but compassionate portrait of an aging nun in a girls' school who cherishes the memory of having taught embroidery to devoted pupils—daughters of flour kings and lumber barons—but who is now reduced to teaching a short course in needlework: "I. Hosiery Mending—a) holes; b) runners; c) preventive measures. II. Buttons. III. Regular Repair—a) the patch. . . ."[59] The story achieves a beautifully balanced ambiguity which simultaneously concedes and laments the necessity of change and progress. It is, in its own way and in its own terms, a feminine companion piece to Powers' "Keystone."

In 1949, Powers reluctantly went to teach for two years at Marquette University in Milwaukee. "When things get really tough I take a job," he said. "Usually teaching. But when I'm teaching, I don't write much. I usually teach creative writing courses, and I read the damned things, the stories, and I sometimes wish that I had that story, because I could do something with it. As a result I don't do my own work. But teaching is better than a lot of things."[60] In order to concentrate on his own writing, he took time off to go to Yaddo again; and there he came to know Theodore Roethke, Marguerite Young, and Robert Lowell. Since then, Lowell has come to regard Powers and Flannery O'Connor as his "two close Catholic writer friends."[61]

In 1951 Powers took his family to live in Greystones, Ireland, an idyllic village in the lovely Wicklow hills beside the sea. The cultural shock and the trials of settling as Americans who were neither rich nor tourists are wonderfully told in two admirable stories by Betty Wahl, "Tide Rips in the Tea Cups" and "The Lace Curtain."[62] But Powers himself, though often amused by the priest-ridden Irishman who goes "arsing along," as Joyce put it, has not felt impelled to use his Irish experiences as subject matter for fiction. Instead, during 1951-52 he completed three stories set chiefly in Minnesota dioceses—"Defection of a Favorite," "The Devil Was the Joker," and "The Presence of Grace."

After two years, Powers took his growing family back to Avon, Minnesota, where they lived with his wife's family until 1956 when the publication of *The Presence of Grace* brought him renewed public notice. He then moved to Milwaukee, from where he commuted to the University of Michigan to teach creative writing again for a semester. Then, early in 1957, he took his family back to Ireland where he settled in a big house in Dalkey and rented a "studio" in Westland Row, Dublin, to work on his novel, *Morte D'Urban*. In a letter to Father Garrelts he wrote, "I arrive at my studio about ten, leave at four, and use it as a base for shopping and auctions . . . My work goes slow, and I must, in a sense, leave it soon to work on a story or two if we are to mobilize again. It's nice to know my literary reputation is rising. Unfortunately, I sold all my shares in that commodity."[63]

Shortly after their fifth child, Jane, was born in Dublin in July, 1958, the Powers family once again returned to the United States—this time to St. Cloud, Minnesota. There he rented a third-floor office, "bare as a monk's cell," above a downtown shoe-store where for three years he worked on *Morte D'Urban*. As a Minneapolis newspaperman described it: "St. Cloud housewives who look out their windows about noon might see this greatest of living story-tellers walking to work six days a week, a sandwich (usually peanut butter and jelly) in his pocket, a thermos of tea under one arm, covering the three-quarters of a mile between home and office in a rapid stride. . . . 'Some days I have a miserable time,' he says. 'I seldom do more than a page in one day. . . . In fact, if I had enough income, I don't think I'd write. It's a sweaty, dirty job.' "[64]

During this period, Powers did not exactly live the life of an ascetic; he remained a devoted family man, and he enjoyed parties and visits from intimate friends. However, the drawn-out illness and death of his dear friend Don Humphrey was an excruciating experience, and it no doubt left its mark on the elegiac conclusion of *Morte D'Urban.* At last, in December, 1961, Powers submitted his completed manuscript, with only minor changes in the chapters that were independently published as short stories.

The publication of *Morte D'Urban* again brought Powers renewed public attention and some refilling of the family coffers—boosted by the sales of paperback editions of *Prince of Darkness* and *The Presence of Grace* and later by the Time Book Club's special edition of stories drawn from both collections. But neither in its American nor various foreign editions did *Morte D'Urban* ever become a runaway best-seller, and Powers was disappointed that the royalties did not enable him to buy a house. But the novel earned him recognition from fellow writers as a major talent; Elizabeth Hardwick (wife of Robert Lowell), Harry Levin, and Gore Vidal chose him (over Katherine Anne Porter, whose *Ship of Fools* also appeared in 1962) as winner of the National Book Award; and the Chicago critics granted him the Thermod Monsen Award for the best book of the year written by a Midwesterner.

"Awards are fine for those writers who get them," Powers said to a New York *Post* reporter. "What do they mean? They mean as much as any public, *official* recognition of a writer's work can mean . . . that he has fooled a hell of a lot of people or that his work is the real thing. I think mine is the latter."[65] How seriously—but whimsically—he considered the power and the glory, and the responsibility of the story-teller is marvelously expressed in his address when he received the National Book Award:

Among my several children there is a little girl, Jane, aged four. The other day she came to me with a piece of paper, a manuscript, her own and I pretended to see words and sentences in her mock handwriting—with which she takes great pains. "Once upon a time," I began. "Long, long ago." After that, there was a moment when I didn't know where I was, but I was relaxed about it, and soon I was reading along, going on about a bear and a dragon who had got into a hell of an argument over which one should be the one to step aside and let the other pass. Jane was absolutely hooked. And why not? A good, strong story line, dialogue, description, and characterization—all excellent. But I was beginning to wonder as the story got better and better, how it would all end. To wonder, yes, and to worry. "And the bear opened his big red mouth," I read, "and the dragon opened his big red mouth"—and right there I came to the bottom of the page. I looked to see if the story was continued on the other side, but it wasn't. Silently I returned the manuscript to the author. She had a stunned look. "*Wait*," she said, and pulling herself together, rushed off to write some more.

There in that little scene, I can see the power and the glory of the story-teller—and the responsibility, in this instance and the responsibility evaded. "The man of letters," Allen Tate has said, "must recreate for his age the image of man, and he must propagate standards by which other men may test that image, and distinguish the false from the true." This, of course, is easier said than done, but this should be the writer's work, always the end in view. Even the ignorant man, if he is an artist, can reach beyond himself. He has the power, in Henry James's words, "to guess the unseen from the seen, to trace the implications of things, to judge the whole piece by the pattern, the condition of feeling life in general so completely that you are well on your way to knowing any particular corner of it." This is the writer's power and glory. But not without responsibility, and this, for the writer, as writer, artist, means responsibility to his craft and therefore to his readers.

When Jane returned with her manuscript, I said, "Oh, yes. Well, the bear opened his big red mouth, yes, *again*, and the dragon opened his big red mouth, *again*, and—and they ate each other up!"

Jane, I could see, didn't care for this at all, and didn't properly understand it. "That was dumb story," she said, but not so much to me as to herself. She was blaming herself.

"No, Jane. That was a very good story," I said, and that, in fact, was how I felt about the story.

And that is how I feel about my novel MORTE D'URBAN, too, but I want to thank the judges, Elizabeth Hardwick, Harry Levin, and Gore Vidal for honoring the book and me as they have.[66]

Flash cameras, press interviews, autograph requests—all the attention and notoriety accorded a celebrity was a heady new experience for Powers; and it seems momentarily to have brought out the Urban in him. No account could possibly communicate the strange intoxication of success better than the letter he wrote on March 21, 1963, to his friend Richard Keefe upon his return from New York to St. Cloud:

Good to hear from you, and I suppose you never expected me to reply, now that I am rich and famous and fly to reel. Actually, I haven't changed so much. There were those days in New York, though, when I was worried—by the change that seemed to be coming over me. . . . I smiled and smiled and bantered and smiled some more and everybody—positively everybody, except for a few people with weak stomachs—loved me. In the end I was glad to go home. Unlike others, I was with myself all the time, and, frankly, I got sick and tired of myself. *Nobody*, I told myself, is such a sweet guy as you're passing yourself off as. But I was still selling, not able to stop all at once, when I reached Chicago, and there, in the few hours I had, I took people to lunch, autographed books (at Marshall Field's and Thomas More's), cut a tape, and in general carried a torch for myself. Yesterday, I gave of my precious time and substance to a reporter and photographer from the Minneapolis newspaper. . . . I was interviewed, blued, and tattooed in New York—no more than that—but I remained on my feet at all times, and won driving. My biggest thrill? Well, I think I'd have to call it meeting Hedda Hopper, rather getting along with her so well. She, as you might know, is also a Doubleday author, and was in town for a few days. She was puzzled that one so young and handsome as I could've written such a fine book (which she hadn't read, by the way), and all I could say by way of explanation, was that it was the result of hard work, clean living, and large advances. I believe it, said Hedda, who asked to meet me again before she retired from the Americana where we of the publishing world were milling around, and after a few more exchanges we parted, with me beseeching her only to stay as she was that night. Had enough?[67]

Shortly after winning the National Book Award, Powers packed up his family and fled back to Greystones, Ireland. In that idyllic retreat (punctuated by occasional visits from Sean O'Faolain and other friends and admirers), he began the slow and painful work on his next novel, *Bill and Joe,* a story of parish life focused on a priest and his curate. His wife, too, after the frustrations and annoyances of settling among the Irish were over, began to write again, and again showed the distaff side of the Powers ironic wit in a magnificent story, "A Shorter History of the Irish People."[68]

With five growing children, the income from *Morte D'Urban* could not stretch beyond two years, even in Ireland, yet Powers rejected a Hollywood option to make a film of *Morte D'Urban;* fearing that the "flicker" merchants would make a farce of the novel. The Ford Foundation awarded him a grant to serve as observer at the Tyrone Guthrie Theater in Minneapolis (the purpose being "to expose established writers in non-dramatic forms to the physical and technical problems of the theater"); but this project, and its fascinating possible consequences in influencing a master of dialogue and situation to turn to a new genre, fell through. Powers then accepted an offer by Smith College in Northampton, Massachusetts, to serve as writer-in-residence for the academic year 1965-66.

III *Occasional Writings*

Apart from his fiction, Powers has from time to time indulged in the writing of didactic little essays, sketches, and dialogues—all of them published in liberal Catholic and secular journals and most of them heavily ironic. Unlike the main body of his work, these do not seem to be carefully revised and they have little merit as literature; however, they do articulate a political and social position which might serve as a frame of reference for the stories.

The earliest of these are two sketches published in *The Catholic Worker* which record observations and meditations during the crisis of faith Powers experienced in 1943: "Night in the County Jail" and "Day in the County Jail." These pieces are remarkable for the quiet calm and restraint which give steely hardness to what might otherwise be merely mushy sentimentality. The narrator of these sketches finds himself enclosed within steel and concrete among ordinary criminals who despised him for being a draft-dodger: "The prisoner next to me called out, 'Hey, Twelve!' several times before I remembered that my cell number was twelve. He wanted to know if I had a match. I told him, no, I was sorry. Then he asked me what they had me in for. I told him simply 'Draft.' He was quiet for a moment. Then I heard him getting a match from the prisoner on the other side of him."[69]

Among these criminals were war veterans—a sailor whose brother had died in his arms at Pearl Harbor and a coast guardsman who had cut the throats of several of the enemy in North Africa; but these men were now in jail for various civil crimes. Powers' explicit moral is quite appropriate to the general outlook of the *Catholic Worker:*

> Here I was in jail because I objected to war, and all about me were men locked up for other reasons. It seemed to me as I listened to these men, that I was surrounded by innocence. I felt old and guilty among them. These men, too, were objectors. They would know that if only they knew themselves. The mild, floundering, tender people, betrayed by leaders, themselves betrayed, the young men marching off to war with books of poetry and New Testaments in knapsacks. They were the leaven. Without them in its armies the war would collapse instantly of its own monstrous evil weight.

In the companion piece, "A Day in the County Jail," Powers records the speech of an eccentric old man, "Pop," who is anxious about his son, a flier home from the Philippines:

> My, but he's had some wonderful experiences. . . . But—and now it was the uneasy tone tending toward sadness—he can't sit still any more, my son just fidgets all the time, has to get up and walk around or go some place and then come home right away so he can go someplace else when he gets there. He never used to be like that. I think sometimes now they're killing my boy and he doesn't even know it. They're killing him, but he just isn't quite dead yet. I think when he dies it'll be so close to the way he is now he won't even know it.[70]

The irony of the earliest piece is compassionate, revealing the pathos of fellow-victims barely aware of the fact that they are victims. But when Powers turned to the victimizers—the condescending do-gooders among the wealthy who were equally unaware that they were victimizers, his irony became more astringent. "A Saint on the Air" is, however, too charged with the moral fervor of Father John Hugo's *Applied Christianity* to be really funny. The radio dialogue between Joy Castleberry, the wealthy socialite engaged in charitable causes, and the eccentric "saint" shows in primitive form the dangers of institutionalized Christian values and the innocent self-betrayal of the smugly self-assured. It is a theme which Powers handles with greater sophistication in later and more mature writings.

> "Do you own your own home?" Joy cut in.
>
> "Of course not. I wouldn't dare. . . . Francis explained all that!"
>
> "All what? Not to me he didn't. Francis who?"
>
> "St. Francis Assisi. They asked him why he didn't get the little brothers organized on a paying basis—more building and some office equipment."
>
> "Well, why didn't he?"
>
> "He knew there would come, sooner or later, the temptation to defend these things by force of arms."

The wit gradually diminishes as the dialogue moves along until the "saint" actually delivers a little sermon on true charity: "It is the mark of real charity that it acts upon the giver. It is the mistake of secular welfare agencies (whom you allow to handle your Charity for you, as though it were dirty laundry) that they regard themselves as technicians whose business it is to prevent acute want. Whereas a Christian, if he is to gain the promised grace connected with good works, must concern himself, not only with the needs of the poor, but with the spirit in which he ministers to them. In short, good works are a privilege, not a necessary evil."[71]

Although Powers has never repudiated these ideas—indeed, they are implicit in all his writings—he never again expressed them so overtly. No doubt his experiences during the war years taught him the futility of sermonizing. From then on his irony became more sustained and sometimes rather shrill, as in "Fun With a Purpose," a description of a fictional address by "America's No. 1 Salesman, Elmer Wheeler, President of Tested Selling Institute, New York":

He said each one of us, if we only knew it, possessed a sizzle. All kinds of sizzles in the world, we all had one, and we all had to find ours. . . . The war had changed a lot of things, including selling. Selling had degenerated during the war. . . . Now things were getting back to normal. With steak plentiful again, it was no longer enough to sell the steak. Now we had to go back to selling the intangible sizzle. A lot of heads were going to fall. Sell the sizzle or starve![72]

A more evenly tempered irony pervades Powers' account of "St. Paul, Home of the Saints." The epigraph of this essay about Minnesota's most Catholic city is taken from *St. Paul: Location, Development, Opportunities* by one F. C. Miller, Ph.D., who neglects to mention that St. Paul is a twin city of Minneapolis, but who points out that it is "very nearly midway between the Prime Meridian and the International Date Line, and enjoys a very central location."[73] Such fatuousness has always amused Powers, and he enjoys poking fun at it. More than any other city, St. Paul serves as the implied capital of the Powers country: isolated from the cultural world (the trip to Minneapolis is long and winding, with stops, starts and portages); proud of its great patron James J. Hill (the robber-baron railroad magnate) but ignorant of its more worthy native son, F. Scott Fitzgerald; predominantly Catholic (a diocesan center with a section known as Vatican City), though with a large Lutheran population once described by Fitzgerald as "righteous, narrow and cheerless, without infinite possibilities for great sorrow or joy." Nevertheless, the accepted religion in St. Paul is really Athleticism: "there is a Bernie Berman hour on the radio during which Saturday's game is prayed over and incense offered."

The essay, a masterpiece of its kind, evokes the scenes and spirit of the city while revealing (chiefly in parenthetical asides) the character of its author. One passage neatly foreshadows the quietly humorous account in *Morte D'Urban* of the naming of Holy Spirit Lake at St. Clement's Hill:

St. Paul rises from the river in a series of hills and valleys. On this Dr. Miller comments: "Some enthusiastic geographers have seriously proposed the substitution of the name of Terrace City." However, between Louis Gaultier, the missionary priest who named the city after the disciple to whom his log chapel was dedicated, resenting the earlier Pig's Eye (after the proprietor of a small saloon), and Archbishop Ireland who built the Cathedral of St. Paul, the enthusiastic geographers have gotten nowhere with their proposal. The city remains Christian in name as it does Catholic in fact.

Such remarks suggest that, despite his amusement at the pretensions and Philistinism of St. Paul, Powers is really rather fond of the place; and he has some good things to say about it: "St. Paul has had good luck with its Archbishops"; "St. Paul lives in retirement and grows older gracefully. Minneapolis will very likely collapse all at once, like a noisy salesman from a heart attack." At heart, Powers remains a profoundly conservative moralist.[74]

The most recent of Powers' occasional satires, a brief playlet called "Moonshot," is about the inane obsessions of the space age. In Act I, a Congressional Committee denies Tom Brown, free-lance astronaut, permission to fly to the moon to test the possibility of constructing buildings there with bricks made of pumice dust and held together with a "waterless cement" obtained from sulphur. In Act II, Tom and his friend Happy, having made the trip in their home-made, supercharged little two-seater, test their theory on the moon. In Act III, after returning to earth, they report their success to the Congressional Committee—but they also warn of the presence of large numbers of *them* on the moon also constructing buildings made of pumice dust. This astounding bit of news unites senators of opposing parties—"whatever our party differences, we never fail to close ranks when threatened from without." The play ends with the astronauts marrying senators' daughters.[75]

There is a certain progression in these incidental writings from a self-conscious, insistent moralizing to a mature and balanced urbanity and, finally, to a kind of scornful contempt. These works may serve to illuminate Powers' fundamental Christian values, his disgust with the American preoccupation with commercial morality and purely sensuous pleasures, and his ridicule of jingoism in the space age.

CHAPTER 2

The World Outside the Rectory

THE POPULARITY of Powers' narratives of rectory life—a subject only he has successfully embodied in American fiction—has unfortunately burdened him with an invidious reputation as a narrow specialist on the priesthood. But, from the very beginning to the publication of *Morte D'Urban,* he has produced magnificent stories on a wide variety of secular themes: a compassionate portrayal of the mind of a European refugee from Fascism ("Renner"); the pathos of old age ("The Old Bird, A Love Story"); the simple-minded saintliness of an exploited domestic ("The Poor Thing"); the innocent victim of ruthless salesmanship in the new suburbs ("Blue Island"); the painful discovery of the inexorable cruelty of nature ("Look How the Fish Live"); a little boy's betrayed adulation of a baseball player ("Jamesie"); and the troubled human values involved in racial hatred and violence ("He Don't Plant Cotton," "The Eye," and "The Trouble"). Had Powers never written a story about a priest, some of these pieces would alone ensure his status as a distinguished writer.

I *Negro Stories*

Powers' five stories on Negro themes—"He Don't Plant Cotton," "The Trouble," "The Eye," "Interlude in a Book Shop," and "The Blessing"—were all written in the early 1940's; and he has confessed that they were written out of "anger at the plight of the Negro."[1] "He Don't Plant Cotton," written in 1942, has as its central character a Negro jazz drummer named "Baby," based on the famous Baby Dodds. This Negro refuses to degrade himself in his own eyes by submitting to the demands of the society around him,[2] but he does not quite have the capacity for pure hatred of the whites as do the piano player, Dodo, and the singer, Libby. Baby resents waiting for streetcars in the cold Chicago winter, playing popular ballads and slick swing tunes instead of honest jazz; but he does it without self-corrosive rancor. A Southern Negro from New Orleans, he paradoxically enjoys lapsing into the Negro stereotype expected of him during the singing of "Ole Man River." When drunken Mississippians at the night club demand that the musicians "tote that bar, lift that bale" all night long, Libby leads the revolt of the performers, and they are fired from their jobs for insulting the customers. When they seek shelter in a store entrance while waiting for a streetcar, only Baby is innocent enough to think that a taxicab would stop for them. A spirit of hope, the undefeated expectation of decency, survives in Baby.

It is prophetic that in Powers' earliest fiction this motif is expressed, for it becomes a recurrent element throughout his literary career; moreover, here, as later, he contrasts it with an all-pervasive corruption in American society. The unique artistry of the Negro is scarcely understood or appreciated, and he is depersonalized in his role as entertainer: Baby's "old tuxedo walked over to the traps. Its black hands rubbed together briskly . . ." (103); and Dodo, too, is dehumanized, reduced to the insect level: "the dim light shaped him into a gigantic, happy spider" (105). The exploitation and humiliation of the Negro by the Southern customers is not only condoned but abetted by the Northern whites: "The manager's voice barked . . . explaining to the gentlemen from Mississippi . . . how it was" (115). Even the Northern intellectuals, the college students who have some sympathy for the Negroes, betray their unconscious racism even when trying to be friendly: "Oh, play it low down, the way *you people* play it" (111).

Finally, unable to endure humiliation any longer, the musicians rebel. "We ain't comin'," Libby said (114), even at the risk of losing their jobs. The rebellion gives them a sense of joy and dignity: "Baby was even a little glad it had happened. A feeling was growing within him that he had wanted to do this for a long time—for years and years, in a hundred different places he had played. . . . Waves of warm exhilaration washed into him, endearing him to himself. No, he smiled, I'm sorry, no favors today" (114-15).

In "He Don't Plant Cotton," Powers poignantly shapes an image of the Negro's long experience of *humiliation* in the North and shows that endurance has its limits. In "The Eye" he takes up the theme of the *violence* which the Negro has endured in the South. The victim is again a Negro musician, Sleep Bailey, a deaf piano player who has heroically rescued a white girl from drowning. To reward him, the girl's boy friend, Clyde Bullen, wants to take up a collection among his friends in the pool hall; but one of them balks, insinuating that the scratches and bruises sustained by the Negro during the rescue is evidence that he had attempted to rape the girl. When a hospital report reveals that the girl is seven months pregnant, a lynch cry is raised; and the mob seeks out Sleep Bailey, who awaits them while calmly playing the piano: "If I'm here I guess I got no call to be scared. . . . Don't it prove nothing if I'm here, if I didn't run away? Don't that prove nothing?" (193). Having been pressured into leading the mob, Clyde Bullen then makes an inchoate, desperate struggle with his conscience and tries in vain to stop the lynching.

Despite the stereotype and stock situations, the story is not without interest. Powers does not focus attention on the innocent victim, but with a certain brute force he employs the device of an internal narrator, Roy, who is a brainless oaf like the barber in Ring Lardner's "Haircut." Like the barber, Roy has no idea of what really happened. It is obvious to the reader, but not to the moronic narrator, that Clyde's refusal to join the chorus of condemnation of the Negro is manifest evidence of his own guilt. Clyde himself is the father of the girl's child, and she was rescued while attempting to drown herself to escape the shame of being an unmarried mother.

Apart from the intricate technique of narrative irony, what is significant is that Clyde does not readily and willingly take up the lynch cry to cover his own responsibility. To be sure, he does not confess his guilt, but neither can he bury it; and he finally turns his fury on the mob in a futile attempt to stop the murder of the Negro. Thus, in an unusual twist away from another stereotype—the Northern liberal's view of the Southern white bigot—Powers presents a conscience-stricken protagonist who cannot escape his own deep-seated morality.

The third of the Negro stories, "The Trouble," also is a first-person narrative dealing with racial violence. One critic, John P. Sisk, has said that "stories of this kind are too easy to handle, coming to the writer, as they do, with too much built-in tension and drama, so that they do not challenge him sufficiently. . . . There is a charge of anger . . . which does him credit as a man but oversimplifies him as an artist."[3] But Sister M. Bernetta Quinn asserts that even more than in some of his rectory tales, Powers achieves "a delicate adjustment of the outer and inner worlds in such a way that, without changing their nature, they can be seen through each other."[4] Sister Bernetta is nearer the truth, for Powers' anger is controlled by a symbolically significant structure and by a rather subtle imagery. Although "The Trouble" may not be entirely successful, it reveals a considerable advance over the earlier Negro stories and distinctly shows Powers moving toward artistic maturity.

The point of view is that of a little Negro boy, a member of a family from New Orleans that has migrated to Chicago in search of employment in the war plants. But Powers ignores the sociological aspects of the wartime race riots to focus on the spiritual crisis of the little boy. He is first shown to be a mischievous child peeking out of the tenement window after his grandmother has told him not to: "she caught us all there and shooed us away and pulled down the green shade. The next time we were real sure she wasn't foxing us before we went to the window and lifted the shade just enough to peek out" (13).

This innocent fun is immediately whiplashed into a vision of horror by the description of brutal murder; but the race riot remains for the boy a spectacle, a macabre entertainment, until the battered body of his mother is carried into the house. The Negro doctor, the boy's father, and then the new parish priest are summoned; but there is some speculation about whether the priest will bother to come—for, as the father says, "his predecessor couldn't stand to save black souls."

From the window the boy watches his grandmother go out at the height of the riot to buy candles; and, to his astonishment, he observes her covertly providing sanctuary to a white man fleeing from a Negro mob. But the father confronts the man with a threat to kill him if the mother dies. Finally the priest arrives, and at that point in the narrative the conflict between the races modulates into a spiritual conflict with the father. The priest's administering the final sacrament influences the boy's father to abandon his threat to kill the loathsome white man: "'I wouldn't touch you.' That was all. He moved slowly back to Mama's bed and his big shoulders were sagged down like I never saw them before" (32).

Both the father and the priest despise the white man, but both manifest the divine injunction, "Be ye angry and sin not: let not the sun go down upon your wrath" (Ephesians 4:26). The presence of grace is in these Negroes; even the little boy's sister Carrie, who had refused to submit to a "white" God, kneels to pray. The change in the father, the final crisis of the story, is foreshadowed by the earlier one in the boy, who at the beginning "wanted to see some whites get killed for a change" (14). He experiences a momentary ambivalence when it appears that his wish may come true and then falls into grace: "I did not see what difference it could make to Mama if the white man lived or died. It only had something to do with us and him. . . . *The trouble* is somebody gets cheated or insulted or killed and somebody else tries to make it come out even by cheating and insulting and killing the cheaters and insulters and killers. Only they never do. I did not think they ever would" (22; italics mine).

When the father too is infused with this spirit, the story, which opened with violence, closes with charity, which "suffereth long, and is kind" (I Corinthian, 13:4). Thus "The Trouble" supports Evelyn Waugh's observation that Powers' "whole art is everywhere infused and directed by his Faith."[5] Even if this story also supports Robert Daniels' complaint that "the Negro stories in particular are badly didactic,"[6] it employs a pattern of animal imagery that indicates a firm artistic control behind the child-narrator's simple idiom. Early in the story, the boy compares the white man to rats, "the biggest live game you can find in ordinary times" (13). Later one of the militant Negroes, quoting Claude McKay, declares: "If we must die, let it not be like hogs hunted and penned in an inglorious spot" (17). When the fleeing white man appears in the alley, he blows a bugle "like the white folks do when they go fox hunting" (20).

But these manifestations of man's animal nature modulate into Christian charity when the priest, Father Crowe (a white man with the name of a black bird), comes to administer Extreme Unction to the dying mother. Such an image pattern in a story written in anger and in one sitting at the typewriter is evidence of Powers' growing skill. Powers himself says of "The Trouble," that "It's not a terribly good story, but it's not a bad story. I don't work like that anymore. Now it takes me a month or two to write a story."[7]

Apart from the three Negro stories which Powers collected in *Prince of Darkness,* there are two which he quite properly omitted. They deserve attention, however, because they anticipate certain themes in his more mature fiction: the morality of everyday life, and the conflict between idealism and practicality within the Catholic Church. The first of these themes is embodied in an early sketch, "Interlude in a Bookshop," which was published in the liberal Negro journal, *Opportunity.* The story shows the moral superiority and the moral victory of the Negro with a levity that foreshadows the wit of Powers' later work. Two moral pigmies, Mr. Flynn, a short man, and Mr. Mosby, a shorter man, find their usual competitive zeal in serving booklovers dampened by the entrance of a Negro woman into the shop. After she buys an inexpensive paperback from the truculent Mr. Flynn, he hands her the unwrapped purchase with a lie:

> "We never wrap small purchases on account of paper shortage."
>
> "That's all right. . . . I can put it right in my bag. Is it severe?"
>
> "What?"
>
> "The paper shortage?"
>
> "Oh, yes, yes indeed." (22)

Mr. Flynn is no match for the perceptiveness and the poise of the woman. When she continues to browse and begins to show signs of becoming a heavy purchaser, Mr. Mosby tries to take over the sale. Eventually, each clerk tries to get in ahead of the other. Flynn wins the sale, but a crisis arises when the woman offers to pay by check. His apprehensions disappear, however, when he notes that the signature on the check is that of a famous Negro opera singer.[8]

Then, Mr. Mosby, seeing an opportunity for revenge, suggests that the opera singer personally autograph a copy of her recently published book for Mr. Flynn. Mosby knows that "poor Flynn would have to buy the book now" (23) and would thus lose whatever commission he made on the sale. This sly trick skews the story away from a final Negro-white confrontation to show how greed and vindictiveness among whites can be even stronger forces than racial prejudice. In the last paragraph, another clerk, the crotchety Mr. Channing, looks into Bartlett's to find a quotation about Fame and Gold o'ercoming all. Although there is nothing especially distinguished about "Interlude in a Bookshop," Powers undoubtedly gained perspective by looking at serious issues from a comic point of view.

Another early story, "Blessing," published in the Catholic monthly *The Sign,* was also omitted from *Prince of Darkness.* Like "The Trouble," it deals with a test of faith in a Catholic Negro family that becomes the victim of racial violence. A Negro boy, converted to Catholicism by a young curate, in turn converts his brothers, sisters, and widowed mother. Though many in the parish clearly resent the presence of Negroes at Mass, the pastor himself determines to give the mother instruction. The children transfer to the parochial school, and the family moves into a run-down house near the church. Frightened by anonymous threats of arson, the mother summons the curate to bless her house; but, just as the blessing is concluded, the dwelling goes up in flames. The curate, undaunted, determines to take the family into the rectory—"if they would come now" (22).

The story is in three parts; the gravest flaw is the shift from scene to summary in part two, which consists of a long, moralistic letter from the curate to his brother, describing his hopes and fears. Of course, the device of the letter is not necessarily in itself a poor technique, but this one introduces its message with the rhetoric one might expect from a callow priest: "I am about to embark upon a subject I've tried, but failed miserably, to be calm about. It is one that concerns all of us Catholics, as such, in this country: mortally" (19). Now this sort of utterance from a character in *Morte D'Urban* would certainly be ironic. When Father Urban says such a thing, he doesn't mean it; and when he becomes the kind of priest who can genuinely mean it, he is no longer able to say it. But Powers' moral fervor in the "Blessing" drives him to use fiction as propaganda for a liberal, humane, and socially-oriented Catholicism, and he loses control as an artist. There is, of course, nothing wrong about the values expressed, but they are *expressed* rather than embodied in art.

Nevertheless, it is instructive to note what values dominate Powers' thought, for he has never repudiated them—he has simply learned to dramatize them more subtly and effectively. Father Blair writes to his brother:

> Here . . . are ten shining souls, brought to their knees not by tyranny, nor clamor nor convention—the dynamics of the day—but rather of their own free will, by a love beyond themselves, for the first and highest purpose, the glory of God. . . . (20)
>
> We have a wisdom which is wiser than the prudence of this world—the folly of the Cross. Let us therefore commit ourselves to a program of Catholic social action which is frankly unwise, incautious, and imprudent by the standards of this world. Let us dare to take Christ literally. Then we shall begin to be great. Let us merit the hatred of the world and of worldly Catholics by advocating full educational equality for colored Catholics. If we are too prudent, too cautious, in a word, too cowardly to do so, then we certainly have no serious belief in the doctrine of the Mystical Body of Christ. (22)

But the "Blessing" does manifest artistic power in other ways: vivid descriptive details ("his sockless toes budding brownly from the ends of his shoes"); dramatic foreshadowings (the flames of the candles in the house during the blessing anticipate and contrast with the cruel, crackling fire that destroys the house); images that communicate more than the central intelligence of the story comprehends ("he saw the streetlight turn yellow, flare up too brightly, and finally go out, leaving the street in darkness" [22]—the arsonists at work have put out the light of faith and reason); and significant realistic details ("As the priest pulled the widow and son out of the burning house, he saw his hat hung within easy reach, but he would not take it and was a little sickened to think he had thought of it at all.") (22)

In this story is the germ of an idea that grew to become one of the most salient features of Powers' most characteristic fiction—the comedy of a pastor's relations with his curate:

> Many people, including priests, do not understand the Pastor (call him strict, anti-social, etc.), but I believe I am beginning to know the man. You may remember my misgivings when I

> learned I was to be his curate at St. Gregory's. He is an implacable enemy to all easy piety, and—should I say, as a consequence?—the most saintly priest I know. I recall the first brush we had. He woke up one morning with a beautiful boil on his neck. I remarked (not in all seriousness) that he was fortunate to have such a boil. Why fortunate? he growled. Suffering is a means to perfection, Father, I replied. Huh! he snorted, I suppose that's why the Bishop sent me you! (23)

In this situation is the beginning of such relationships as those of Father Burner and Father Malt in "Prince of Darkness," Father Fabre and his pastor in "The Presence of Grace" and "A Losing Game," Father Udovic and the Bishop in "Dawn," Father Early and the Bishop in "Zeal," and of Bill and Joe in the novel.

II *Anti-Semitism*

As an intense young liberal in the early 1940's, Powers was, of course, concerned with social issues other than the Negro problem. His one story dealing with the problem of the Jews, "Renner," is so atmospheric and suggestive that the reviewer for the London *Times Literary Supplement* found it the only story in *Prince of Darkness* in which "the author's subtlety of approach obscures his intention."[9] The story is subtle, but not obscure; and it is an immensely superior work of art in comparison to any of the Negro stories. It requires more concentrated attention and more astuteness from the reader before it yields its force and meaning.

"Renner" is several stories merged into one, a brilliant, unified complexity showing Fascism in the drama of everyday life—in the present and the past, in Europe and America. As the narrator says of the anti-Semites, "such men are everywhere, never without a country" (147). For the first time in Powers' fiction, an internal narrator approaches intelligence, maturity, and perceptiveness, but ultimately even he cannot fully understand the experience thrust before his consciousness from worlds he has never known. For an hour or so, he sits with his friend Renner in a cozy German restaurant with a gay-90's decor which evokes images of a happy world that exists only in the illusions of the present. Looking at the paintings on the wall, Renner says, "Because he could paint like that, . . . my uncle became president of the Vienna Academy"; and it is gradually revealed that the pleasant part of that other world is also an illusion.

The narrator is confronted with two lines of force that move through the story: (1) the ongoing drama of the present—Emil, the proprietor of the restaurant with his card-playing friends reacting to a Jewish businessman who comes in for dinner; and (2) the autobiography of Renner, an Austrian exile from Fascism who encounters virulent forms of it in the United States. The climax of the story occurs when these two narrative lines collide; but the meaning of that impact is left implicit: men of good will are confused and powerless in a world without Christian values.

As the story opens, the narrator reveals that he had never known the "good old days" evoked by their setting, but he observes that among the "swillish brown paintings" of fat tippling friars in cellars and other subjects there are "no fishes on platters" (143). Thus the opening paragraph suggests the paradox of appearance and reality, for the surface display of geniality obscures the absence of Christianity. The narrator is only partially aware of—indeed, morally indifferent to—the significance of what he sees and hears. For example, he notes that there was "something dimly sinister about Emil" (144), the proprietor, but he fails to probe for it. Later, he says: "On occasion I had wondered whether Renner was Jewish, always half-heartedly, so that I forgot what I was wondering about, and it would be a while before I wondered again" (148). In ordinary social situations such indifference might be to the narrator's credit; here it suggests a desire to avoid difficulties.

This pusillanimous narrator ("When Emil brought our glasses back. . . I became preoccupied with a button on my coat" [144]) rarely makes pointed judgments about the people and events he observes; more often than not, he merely mulls over Renner's comments. For example, when Renner says, "An age-old alliance, . . . the Irish and the Germans," he considers the question ("There was, in fact, a rough unity about them") until he reaches the conclusion: "One thing was sure: they all *belonged*" (151-52). But he does not realize that those who belong, who occupy the inner sanctums of society everywhere and are therefore corrupt, inevitably defeat the kind, the gentle, and the good. The very setting of the story, the restaurant, is a place where poets and artists used to gather; but now the crude card players have displaced them in the "erstwhile hearth of the nation's literary great" (152).

Behind the narrator, of course, is Powers, who causes the story to move in alternate rhythmic pulses of time toward its climax when Renner's sudden gesture of indignation at the card players freezes in paralysis and defeat. The narrative movement toward that closure is intricately structured: (1) five episodes of the present alternate with five episodes of Renner's past; (2) then a brief abstract discussion of Christianity, followed by (3) Renner's account of the immediate past event that triggers the climax in the present. The structure might be diagrammed as follows:

PRESENT
(scenes in restaurant)

(1)	(2)	(3)	(4)	(5)
Description of setting and Emil	Enter Mr. Ross	Mr. Ross orders	Mr. Ross served	Mr. Ross departs

DISCUSSION OF CHRIST
Renner explodes at anti-Semites

PAST
(scenes in Renner's life)

Hitler and art in Vienna early 1920's	Geometry teacher at school	Renner victim of spy	Renner recalls super's head	Renner's wife flees; he follows, finds USA unfriendly

DISCUSSION OF CHRIST
Renner explodes at super

This alternation of the American present with the European past emphasizes the similarity in the moral corruption of the two areas as if to say that chauvinism, the rejection of foreigners, and the mockery of Jews lead everywhere to the same spiritual rottenness. For example, the fanatic nationalism of Renner's Austrian geometry teacher reminds the narrator of a line from

James Thomson's *The Seasons:* "Delightful task . . . to rear the tender thought, to teach the young idea how to shoot" (146-47). Stalin violates his own ban on American imports to smoke Edgeworth pipe tobacco, and the English harry foxes and horses. It is in such small hypocrisies and not in "the eternal traffic jams of empires" (154) that the mature Powers finds the most intense moral significance. Renner, whose wife's lament had been that "nothing roused him" (154), has come to learn that he must rebel—and must be defeated: "Martyrdom, indecent as it sounds to our itching ears, is not supposed to be too much to suffer for it [Christ's law]" (155). But few are prepared to suffer such a fate; most men succumb to another "supernatural element, which . . . goes by the name of Pressure from Above" (157).

Two climactic events cap the story. First is Renner's account of the "little three-act tragedy" which took place earlier that afternoon at the small "war" plant (manufacturing ashtrays and picture frames) where both Renner and the narrator have been employed. One of the workers, Victoria Marzak, had demanded better working conditions in the stock room; but when the super had shamed her for complaining "when there were boys dying in fox-holes" (156), Victoria had wilted and gone back to her job. "But tell me," says the narrator, "what was the foolish thing you did in the second act?"

> "I stood up to the super and told him a few things, mostly concerning the rights and dignity of man."
>
> I considered the implications of this for a moment. "Then, as we say, you are no longer with the company?"
>
> "Yes."
>
> "You were fired?"
>
> "Yes. Insubordination." (157)

The final climax occurs after the flamboyant Mr. Ross heavily tips the unctuous Emil and departs. One of the card players, attempting Yiddish dialect, says, "So that was Mr. Ross" (158). This is hardly a brutal manifestation of anti-Semitism, but to Renner, if not to the narrator, it is nevertheless the corrupt source from which synagogue-burning, pogroms, and genocide emerge:

> Abruptly Renner stood up, jolting our table sharply, his face all swollen and red, and started across the floor. Before I could get up and interfere, he came to a wavering halt. Looking at him were four surprised faces and there seemed to be nothing about them familiar or hateful to Renner. Evidently he was bewildered to find no super: he had seen his head a moment before. He gave me an ashamed look which was not without resentment. Then he walked back to our table, stuck his pipe, which was lying there, in his pocket, threw down some money, and went out the door. (159)

Once again, Renner is a man on the run after an impotent, futile gesture. It is important, however, that Renner's sense of outrage *not* be misinterpreted as the personal resentment of a Jew. For one thing, Powers deliberately makes Renner's racial identity a matter of no importance, implying that any decent man's gorge would rise at such a slimy display of racial prejudice. For another, Renner's climactic act was preceded by the little tragedy of the afternoon in which his defense of the "rights and dignity of man" had nothing to do with racial problems (158). Furthermore, the largest conceptual frame for the episodes and ideas of the story is, however obliquely presented, religious.

The first religious reference in the story is casual enough, but it alerts us to the fact that the narrator must be a Catholic, and a naïve one at that. Upon learning that Renner's uncle had been president of the Vienna Academy of Art, he muses: "Achievement through violence or succession or cunning or even merit is common enough. But president of an academy of art—now there was an inscrutable honor, beyond accounting for, like being an archbishop (except in Italy), only more so" (145). Among other relations, this passage reaffirms our awareness of the narrator's relative naïveté; for, as Powers' other stories show, "cunning or even merit" is often the factor that determines status in religious hierarchies. The narrator says of Renner, "his species, spiritually speaking, tends to make itself at home in exile" (148); but it is obvious that Renner will never be at home anywhere since he cannot limit his Christianity to "the community fund, doing good, and brisk mottoes on the wall." All these, Renner says, are ways of "copulating with circumstance" (155).

Renner knows how the Christian tradition has become debased

in American society. His account of the way Victoria Marzak was defeated in her tiny struggle for human decency is a tour de force of sustained religious irony:

> "Act Three was classic, revealing the history of human progress, or the effects of original sin (reason darkened), depending on your taste in terminology. The super introduced Victoria to the supernatural element, which in our department goes by the name of Pressure from Above. He invoked pressure as the first cause of all conditions, including working. In short, the less said about conditions the better. Victoria wilted. But pressure, besides being a just and jealous god, is merciful. The super forgave her trespasses, said he was working on a raise for her, and she went back to her job (under the same conditions), beating her sizable breast and crying *mea culpa* for having inveighed against them—conditions, that is—as things sacred to Pressure. Curtain." . . . "In case you are wondering," Renner continued, "Victoria represents suffering humanity suffering as it was in the beginning, is now, and ever shall be, world without end." (157-58)

With this conviction and with the awareness that the card players are merely the super multiplied, Renner's urge is to protest. To be sure, Mr. Ross is not "suffering humanity"—not yet. Pompous, condescending, and ostentatiously well-to-do, he is hardly a man to inspire the martyrdom of others on his behalf. But the card-playing Entrepreneur does not merely mock Mr. Ross, he mocks Jewishness. And Renner is not roused to defend Mr. Ross, he is urged to attack a contemptible and potentially dangerous manifestation of anti-Semitism. Yet Renner, paralyzed by a realization of the futility of his intended act, comes to a wavering halt before the surprised faces of the card players. He knows that the super was indeed present in the persona of the Entrepreneur. Super, Entrepreneur, der Fuehrer—all exert a God-mocking Pressure from Above. Renner had just a few hours earlier seen once again, after a lifetime of such experiences, what "ever shall be." Nevertheless, he feels shame at his failure and resentment at the narrator's complacency before he departs in anger, leaving behind the narrator whose impulse was to rise, not to join his friend in a showdown with bigotry but to prevent an embarrassing scene.

There is an immense poignancy to Renner's experience, a poignancy contained by the narrator's self-control, his avoidance of excess emotion, his evasion of embarrassing confrontations, and his willingness to compromise: "I told Emil the beer was good, very—when he waited for more—very good beer" (156). The poignancy is also paradoxically both tempered and heightened by the ironic wit: "It's too bad der Fuehrer couldn't paint a little. Another bad painter, we could have stood that. . . . The Austrian army was not the most formidable in the world, except of course at regimental balls" (144), the geometry teacher would "get furious and throw the squares and triangles at the pupils" (146). This is the same ironic technique that is handled with sustained power in the later stories and in *Morte D'Urban.*

III *Age and Youth*

"The Old Bird, A Love Story" is, among the ten pieces that Powers published in the years 1943-45, remarkable for its quiet restraint and dignity, its controlled evocation of pathos, its gentle insight into the marital love of the aged. It has no black wit, no scorching irony, no inflamed, reformist zeal, no didactic rhetoric. It is strange to find this work among the early stories—strange but satisfying—because it confirms the observation that Powers began as a pure artist as well as a social reformer. Fortunately, the artist in him eventually triumphed. More than any other story in *Prince of Darkness,* "The Old Bird" exemplifies one reviewer's observation that "the expert technique of these stories is as unemotional and photographic as the later Hemingway, consisting mainly of placing the model in a clear light and shooting."[10]

"The Old Bird" depicts a day in the life of an old man, Mr. Newman, who, although he has a horror of intruding where he isn't wanted, is driven by the approach of Christmas to seek a job. After running the gauntlet of the information girl, the employment interviewer, and the boss of the shipping department, he puts in an exhausting day's work and returns home to his sympathetic wife. As this summation indicates, the story is not a powerfully dramatic narrative but a poignant character study built up with sensitively observed details. In his encounter with the information girl, "for all his show of business, almost brusqueness, he radiated timidity" (197). Mr. Newman feels too old to be of any use to the company. Filling out his application form with his ancient orange fountain pen, he suddenly fears that his green ink may jeopardize his chances of a job. He is able to decipher PRSNLTY as "personality," but is stumped by NTC ("neurotic"?).

Quite agitated, he is ushered into the office of Mr. Shanahan, the interviewer: "Mr. Shanahan, his eyes . . . reading the letter, noiselessly extended a hand toward Mr. Newman. A moment later he moved his head and it was then that Mr. Newman saw the hand. Mr. Newman paled. Caught napping! A bad beginning. He hastened to shake Mr. Shanahan's hand, recoiled in time. Mr. Shanahan had only been reaching for the application. Mr. Newman handed it to Mr. Shanahan and said, 'Thank you,' for some reason" (201). Such skill in looking simultaneously at and through Mr. Newman is impressive. The humor mocks with compassion.

Because of the wartime labor shortage, Mr. Newman is hired —not for office work, as he had hoped, but in the shipping room. However, as the elevator descends, his spirit sinks as he learns that the job doesn't pay much at the beginning but that the name of the firm would make it easier for him to find another position should he leave this one; and, "out of the elevator and in the lower depths, Mr. Shanahan said he would like to make sure Mr. Newman understood the job was only temporary" (203). Then, Mr. Newman suffers one humiliation after another at the hands of Mr. Hurley; he manages to get through the day to head for home in a mood "unfamiliar to him, one of achievement and crazy gaiety" (209).

This mood is dissipated, however, by the heavy snows, the crowded streetcars, and his confusion in trying to find a way of telling his wife of his success—and failure. He confronts "the truest condition of their married life. . . . She was the audience . . . and he was always on stage, the actor who was never taken quite seriously by his audience, no matter how heroic the role" (212). He shamelessly exaggerates the fine qualities of the old-line firm that had hired him, only to have his fantasies collapse with her enthusiastic response: "Then maybe they'll keep you after Christmas, Charley!" Because she loves him and understands him, she does not challenge his inept lie: "Yes. You know, I think they will. I'm sure of it" (214). And, as in the poignant conclusion of Joyce's "The Dead" and Powers' own "Lions,

Harts, Leaping Does," "Snowflakes tumbled in feathery confusion past the yellow light burning in the court, wonderfully white against the night, smothering the whole dirty, roaring, guilty city in innocence and silence and beauty" (213). As Marcus Klein says of Nabokov's short stories, "There is the rare accuracy, just so much of sorrowing and just so much of scrutiny, which is what we mean by compassion."[11]

But such a delicate balance of sorrowing and scrutiny is lacking in "Jamesie," Powers' autobiographical narrative about a nine-year-old boy who discovers that his idol is corrupt. The story has invited comparison with Hemingway's "My Old Man" and with Sherwood Anderson's "I Want to Know Why." Its motif is one which has attracted almost every significant American writer since Hawthorne's "My Kinsman, Major Molineux." But "Jamesie" is not a distinguished piece of work, probably because a young writer looking back on his own boyhood cannot achieve sufficient psychic distance and control to shape his materials into genuine art. Powers himself has confessed to a certain embarrassment at the obvious autobiographical elements, most prominent of which are his own name and the town in which he was born (Jayville is Jacksonville).

It is difficult to shape a richly textured emotional experience in the perspective and idiom of a boy. In Faulkner's "That Evening Sun," Lionel Trilling's "The Other Margaret," and Robert Penn Warren's "Blackberry Winter," that difficulty is avoided by making the initiation into evil a reminiscence or an observation of a sophisticated adult. Another difficulty when the central intelligence of the story is much less perceptive than the reader is an anti-climactic conclusion. Faulkner and Warren succeed by employing a rich symbolism and by introducing elements of complex atmosphere and threatened violence; Trilling, by making the child's discovery parallel that of a concomitant discovery by the adult. Hemingway and Anderson are superior in that they create a tension between a stronger drama of corruption and a taut, slangy prose style. But Powers, by keeping everything simple and ordinary, both in event and narrative technique, must finally rely on sentimentality.

The plot of "Jamesie" is simple. A boy—whose father, a Coolidge man, can't think of anything else to do on Sundays but "a visit to the office, fixing up his mother's grave in Calvary, or just sitting on the porch with all the Chicago papers" (71)—lives in a rich fantasy world of baseball fact and fiction. In that world powerful gambling interests are always bribing players to throw a crucial game; but, as Jamesie comes to realize, it is only in the *Baseball Bill* books that the hero has moral stamina to resist. When Jamesie's idol, Lefty, is arrested for collusion with gamblers, he refuses to believe the charge is true. That evening he sulks in his room and has a cruel set-to with his kind Aunt Kate.

The next morning he visits Lefty in jail: "Wasn't that the odor of strong drink and cigar smoke—" he asks himself, in the idiom of Baseball Bill. "He gave up, he knew now. . . . Jamesie got his legs to take him away, out of the jail, around the corner. . . . He did not go through alleys, across lots, between buildings, over fences. No. He used streets and sidewalks, like anyone else, to get where he was going—away—and was not quite himself" (99).

John P. Sisk has, in effect, linked "Jamesie" with Powers' earlier stories by his observation that "implicitly or explicitly the literature of innocence is social criticism."[12] Such a flat pronouncement is contradicted by such stories as Hawthorne's "Roger Malvin's Burial" and "My Kinsman, Major Molineux" and Graham Greene's "The Basement Room," where the evil that shatters innocence is either personal or cosmic, but not—strictly speaking—social. Nevertheless, Sisk's observation is appropriate to "Jamesie," a narrative in which perhaps the only subtle element is the implicit suggestion that in an American milieu, corrupted by the commercial ethic, it is not surprising that Lefty should prove vulnerable.

In cheap fiction Baseball Bill cannot be induced to throw the World Series, but in the real world Lefty's defection reminds Uncle Pat of the Black Sox Scandal of 1919. Jamesie himself is lured into petty violations of good form in his business enterprises: he sells out his copies of *Liberty* magazine and delivers a copy marked "sample" to a regular subscriber; he buys six boxes of his own supply of Rosebud salve in order to win a premium. The paradoxical world he lives in is neatly expressed on the card Jamesie gets from a weighing machine: "Cultivate your good tastes and make the most of your business connections" (95).

And in other ways Powers also captures the idea that the commercial temptations of the flesh are always more exciting than the dullness of moral order: "The calliope . . . had roamed the streets, all red and gold and glittering like a hussy among the pious, black Fords parked on the Square, blaring and showing off, with a sign, Jayville vs. Beardstown" (76). However deftly the evil of Lefty is shown to be consonant with the evils of the larger society in which it occurs, and however felicitously the attractions of that evil may be expressed in an occasional image, the language and the dramatic structure of "Jamesie" are at best mediocre. Neither can be compared, for example, with these qualities in "The Trouble," which remains artistically and morally Powers' only worthy contribution to the literature of young innocence encountering evil.

IV *Friends and Neighbors*

In the first five years of his career, culminating with the appearance of *Prince of Darkness* in 1947, ten of the sixteen pieces which Powers published were secular in theme, setting, and characters. But the religious stories were generally far superior as literary art, and Powers turned his attention more and more to scenes of clerical life. In fact, only two of the nine stories in his second collection, *The Presence of Grace* (1956) are secular—"The Poor Thing" and "Blue Island." Both of them are superior to all the earlier secular stories, with the exception of "Renner," and they are equal to the best of the religious stories in that collection.

As Donald Barr commented, "where in the earlier book he dealt often with the shock and humiliation of Negro life, in this book (for instance, in 'Blue Island,' about a couple who try to get accepted in a small town, while they are tormented by private shames like itches they dare not scratch in public) the terrors are the subtle terrors of gentility, and the pity is for the precious and spurious."[13] Blue Island is not a small town, but a suburb of Minneapolis where Ralph Davicci, a liquor dealer and proprietor of cheap bars, has installed his pregnant bride Ethel. Lonely and eager for the approval of their upper middle-class neighbors, they easily fall victim to Mrs. Hancock, a sordid female who, under the guise of arranging a get-together coffee hour, uses their home to stage a party for selling kitchen utensils.

As a sociological study of class disorientation and alienation, "Blue Island" is easily the equal of anything by, say, John O'Hara; but as a work of art it is far superior. Written with a Joycean scrupulous meanness, "Blue Island" is actually the sustained interior monologue of Ethel Davicci who, despite her life among the riffraff, remains a well-meaning, good-hearted, dumb blonde. Ethel is alert to the possibility of danger, oblivious of the real tactics of Mrs. Hancock, and gradually caught in her clutches. Here Powers' subtle technique of implications requires the closest possible attention of the reader, as the following annotated passage will show:

> Mrs. Hancock had guessed right about Ethel and Ralph, that they were newly-weds. [The syntax is Ethel's, as is the naïveté which prevents her from realizing that Mrs. Hancock had guessed no such thing, but was following a sales lead.] "Am I right in thinking you're of Swedish descent, Mrs. Davicky? You, I mean?" [Mrs. Hancock, who cannot properly pronounce a familiar Italian name, makes a subtle appeal to possible feelings of ethnic superiority in Ethel. She cannot know that Ethel has a family problem of a different order.]
>
> Ethel smiled, as if taking a compliment, and said nothing. [The smile and the silence are practiced defensive tactics in coping with the problem.]
>
> "I only ask because so many people in the neighborhood are. [Which falsely suggests that Mrs. Hancock is of the neighborhood and raises Ethel's confidence in the possibility of establishing ties with the others.] I'm not myself," said Mrs. Hancock. [Suggesting that if *she* has been able to succeed without such an advantage, Ethel will have no trouble at all.] She was unnaturally pink, with tinted blue hair. [Ethel's simple observation, without awareness of the sinister implications of the unnatural.] Her own sharp-looking teeth were transparent at the tips. "But you're so fair." [Luscious enough to bite into?]
>
> "My maiden name was Taylor," Ethel said. It was, and it wasn't–it was the name she'd got at the orphanage. [She fears that a questionable lineage might prove to be a handicap and has developed tactics of concealment short of outright lying.] (147)

And so, throughout the story, one finds not merely a realistic description of a milieu and dialogue, as in O'Hara, but a presentation closer to Joyce's techniques of implication in *Dubliners.*

The story has four parts: (1) Ethel's encounter with Mrs. Hancock and the invitations to the coffee hour, (2) Ralph's anxiety over the success of the affair—and exposition accounting for that anxiety, (3) preparations, (4) the debacle of the coffee hour and its aftermath. The aftermath concludes with the arrival of Ralph, who had apparently been hovering nervously and solicitously in the background: "He was carrying a big club of roses" (162). This last image embodies a powerful epiphany, serving the same function as "I'll say a *Hail Mary*" at the end of Joyce's "Counterparts" or "Now there would be time for everything" at the end of Katherine Anne Porter's "Pale Horse, Pale Rider."

Had the story been simply another sophisticated *New Yorker* hatchet job on life in the new suburbs, it could have ended with Ethel's discovery of the nausea of her neighbors who clearly resented being tricked into serving as a captive audience for a Shipshape utensils saleswoman: "In a minute, she'd have to get up and go down to them and do something—but then she heard the coat hangers banging back empty in the closet downstairs, and the front door opening, and finally, closing. There was a moment of perfect silence in the house before her sudden sob . . ." (161).

That is clearly a satisfactory point of closure. But Powers follows it with Ethel's final dialogue with Mrs. Hancock and Ralph's arrival. Thus the ending of part four nearly parallels the ending of part one. Yet the gain of narrative power does not derive merely from the structural parallel; more important is that last line about his "carrying a big club of roses." It reveals in a flash that Ralph, not Mrs. Hancock, is ultimately responsible for these events. In his excess zeal for status and acceptance in a milieu utterly foreign to his own heritage or to his wife's personality, he has created the situation that has made misery inevitable. He has clubbed her with inept kindness.

That denouement explains and justifies the large role that Ralph plays in the middle two acts of this pathetic little domestic drama. The exposition in part two is smoothly introduced as Ethel considers how Ralph has changed since they moved to Blue Island. Formerly a happy extrovert, he is now tense and inhibited: "He should relax and take the neighbors as they came.

Or move . . . She didn't know why they were there when they could just as well be living at Minnetonka or White Bear, where they could keep a launch like the one they'd hired in Florida—and where the houses were far apart and neighbors wouldn't matter so much. What were they waiting for? (153). . . . Ethel didn't ever want to see that sick look of Ralph's on a child of hers" (155).

Ralph Davicci had renounced his own Italian family and his nickname of "Rocky," and he had ceased being a practicing Catholic; he dressed too ostentatiously well; he attempted to play golf and read the *Reader's Digest*; and he pressed his wife into a life for which she was not suited. The whole episode of the coffee hour and of Ethel's failure is therefore merely an oblique way of understanding the inevitable wrong of a man's not being true to himself. Ethel and Mrs. Hancock are antagonists, and Ethel is the ironically conceived central intelligence; but Ralph Davicci is the protagonist and the ultimate cause of the events.

Sister M. Bernetta Quinn is mistaken in her notion that "Blue Island" is the only story in *The Presence of Grace* that "has no explicit religious references."[14] To be sure, the fact that Ralph does not attend church is cited only once, but this important detail reveals that Ralph is alienated from himself. John P. Sisk has observed that both "Blue Island" and "The Poor Thing," two stories in which naïveté and indecision make one an easy victim of the machinations of others, "end in a kind of darkness that is unusual in Powers."[15] The explanation may lie in Powers' firm conviction that "you can't win in this world. In my secular stories this world is the only one there can be, but in the clerical stories there is always the shadow of another world."[16] Considered in this larger perspective, the apostasy of Ralph Davicci is no longer a minor matter; in terms of the grand design of the whole of Powers' fiction, it explains everything.

In "The Poor Thing" Catholicism plays a more prominent role than in "Blue Island," which means that the astringency of the irony is increased. The Daviccis' failure to upgrade their social status is pathetic, but at least Ralph's commitment to social success was not hypocritical. However, when a character like Dolly in "The Poor Thing" professes to be a pious Catholic while actually sucking the lives out of all who come within reach of her wheelchair, the quality of the rendered experience isn't so much pathos as it is a kind of dumb amazement at the enormity of petty moral corruption. Apart from the Catholic element, the interpersonal actions of the two stories are quite similar: for selfish reasons, a petty power figure (Ralph Davicci, Mrs. Shepherd) manipulates a well-meaning, weak, decent human being (Ethel, Teresa) into the clutches of a moral monster (Mrs. Hancock, Dolly).

Teresa, an elderly retired spinster with an inadequate pension, is cajoled by Mrs. Shepherd—a bad shepherd leading her sheep to a fleecing—into "temporarily" accepting a position as companion to Dolly, a lifelong invalid, penny-pincher, and emotional leech. Even Teresa's unusual patience cannot endure the bizarre demands and indignities heaped upon her by the invalid, and she quits the job—only to be tricked, in a whiplash conclusion, into returning. The final irony is that the poor thing is Teresa and not the invalid Dolly. Once again, Powers reverses the stereotypes: priests are not always priestly; athletes, not always good sportsmen; Southerners, not always racial bigots eager for a lynching; and the invalid, not always a pitiful creature.

But the impact of this story does not depend solely upon the reversal of stock responses, which is simply an old O. Henry trick. Here Powers plumbs the depths of Catholic moronia and pulls up nauseating images from the sediment, and he does so with a precision and economy of effort that keeps the artistic gesture clean. For example:

> Once, when he [the priest] was there, Teresa had heard Dolly confess, "I missed my morning prayers two times, Father."
>
> "Is that all?"
>
> "Is that all!"
>
> The next time Dolly complained about the priest's not coming often enough, Teresa said, "If you told him half the things you do, you wouldn't want him to come so often. You never think to tell him all those mean things you say about the woman across the way. Don't forget Our Lord was a Jew."
>
> "Teresa! Our Lord was a Galilean. . . ." (55)

Furthermore, the central character is not the invalid; it is Teresa, who resembles the humbler, more recent St. Therese de Lisieux, the simple nun canonized in 1925, rather than the great mystic of Avila. St. Therese was considered remarkable for her childlike simplicity, exemplifying the "little way," achieving goodness by performing the humblest deeds and by carrying out the most trivial actions. When, at the end of the story, Dolly greets Teresa with the ironic epithet, "You poor thing!," it is not merely her hypocrisy that must be observed, for the epithet would be applied even to St. Therese by many even more perceptive than Dolly. By the highest Catholic standards, implicitly evoked in the story, Teresa is not merely a soft touch; in many respects, she approaches saintliness.

However, Teresa does not quite achieve saintliness because she is, to a certain extent, trapped and corrupted by her own pride and her material needs. Once before, Mrs. Merck had discovered her weakness and had literally bribed her into betraying her fellow workers at the store (as did Victoria Marzak in "Renner"). Unlike the saint whom she resembles, she does adjust to circumstances which she is powerless to change; but her heart and most of her deeds are kind and charitable. Her moral character is left for the reader to determine for himself because, even on the level of the ordinary realism, Powers eschews direct comment.

In fact, he never so much as labels the significance of speech or gesture, with a revealing adjective. The inescapable consequence is often an ambiguity for which there is no authorial resolution. For example, one can see in the opening dialogue Mrs. Shepherd's cynical manipulative skill applied to the humble dignity and innate piety of Teresa, but Teresa's own lack of candor makes it a confrontation of two variables:

> "You know, Mrs. Shepherd, I don't have to work."
> "My dear, I know you don't. You just want to supplement your income."
> "Yes, and I like to be doing something."
> "My dear, I know how you feel."
> "And I'm down for light sewing."
> "Of course you are. I don't know whatever made me think of you for this—except they want a nice, refined person that's a Catholic."

The "Dolly" to whom Teresa becomes companion is a plastic, inhuman contrivance—a thing of wires and flexes who is not genuinely aware that she possesses a soul: "The poor thing who met Teresa at the door in a wheelchair wore an artificial flower in her artificial hair" (47). She has a bad habit of giggling slightly and pushing up her wig, inch by inch, showing more and more scalp. This grotesque creature with the baby face spends hours listening to soap operas on the radio and keeping books on the indulgences she gains through her special devotions. That this is a form of living death is reinforced by Dolly's inordinate interest in death—in cancer and the "leopard colonies" (49) where "one by one, their members fall off" (52). Again and again she cajoles Teresa into telling the story of how she got her first raise, chiefly because she is fascinated by the conclusion: "For Teresa the story ended in the raise and promotion, not in her succession to the throne on Miss Merck's death or the cause of it" (52).

Dolly, however, is not so much evil as simply moronic. She *means* to be a pious, sentimental Catholic, but her way of expressing it is unbelievably stupid. In fact, it is a real challenge to Powers' daring and ingenuity to present one of Dolly's poems:

A sight more lovely and sweet
Nowhere on earth have I seen
Than the little bundles of meat
In Mother's arms I mean. (57)

The fact that Teresa kept this poem—the only one she did keep—confirms that even grotesquerie will not repel her from sentimental values. Horrible as she is, Dolly is nevertheless a pathetically dependent human being whom no saintly person can utterly reject. The enormity of the lie that provokes Teresa into returning to her is in itself a measure of Dolly's desperate need. But her return to Dolly, too, is ambiguous because Teresa is coerced into it by the fact that she has been accused of theft, cannot get a reference from Dolly, and is thus at the mercy of the employment agency. Hence, the pious conclusion is leavened by the iron demands of realism.

Powers seems frequently drawn to poignant or sentimental situations, but he is utterly unable to present them in sentimental terms. There is, for example, none of the pathos of Steinbeck's *paisanos*, or the cuteness of O'Hara's Pal Joey. At the very least, there is a certain restraint, detachment, and matter-of-factness, as in "The Old Bird"; more often there is a frame of dead-pan, mock-ironic humor, as in "The Poor Thing." But Powers' astringent wit does not negate sentiment; rather, it controls the qualities of character and situation which in lesser hands would degenerate into sentimentality. One of the most effective means by which Powers avoids mushiness is by removing himself from the story and letting it be simply the record of what transpires in the mind of a character. And one of the means by which he gains astringency and irony is by compressing and abruptly juxtaposing in a jarring rhythmic progression the observations and experiences of his central intelligence.

In that way, he can unemotionally display the dignity of Negro musicians who reach their limit of compromise, the compassion of a wife for her aging husband, the anguish of a boy discovering evil, the indignation of a refugee at a demonstration of racial prejudice, or the saintliness of a simple woman who serves the needs of an invalid moron. The character from whose point of view Powers projects these experiences is, in the collected stories, never one who fully understands and articulates the meaning of that experience. If not a child, an adolescent, or a moron, the narrative medium is usually, like the priest in "The Blessing" or the refugee's friend in "Renner," a person somehow incapable of imagining or perceiving the full significance of evil about him.

V *Nature*

However, in Powers' most recent secular story, "Look How the Fish Live," which appeared in 1957 after the publication of *The Presence of Grace*, the narrative mind is more probing, more meditative than usual. Like Elwin in Trilling's "The Other Margaret" or the schoolteacher in Katherine Anne Porter's "Holiday," the central intelligence of this story actively pursues the meaning of the experience he is undergoing—and achieves insight after considerable struggle to ward it off. Without a trace of the high hilarity or the hard ironic humor of his other stories, "Look How the Fish Live" is sustainedly sad. George Scouffas says that it "comes perhaps closest of all his stories to overt despair over the human condition";[17] and Scouffas is right because, for the first and only time, the protagonist is not only caught in the grip of unalterable cosmic circumstances but is fully aware of it.

Appropriately for a meditative story, the pace is very slow. Each sequence of action and dialogue is followed by the narrator's pondering the significance of it. But again Powers characteristically probes a tremendous issue in homely, modest terms. Powers is outside the grand tradition in American literature, which presents man's confrontation with nature in terms of the huge, wild creatures of the wilderness or the sea. The heroes of *Moby Dick, The Bear,* and *The Old Man and the Sea* are all displaced from the normal, day-to-day milieu; but Powers in "Look How the Fish Live" is working in a smaller and more recent movement, which includes such stories as Sherwood Anderson's "The Egg," Katherine Anne Porter's "The Grave," and William Goyen's "The White Rooster"—stories which dramatize man's conflict with nature in civilized environments. And the familiar environment paradoxically heightens rather than diminishes the horror and the anguish (just as man's inhumanity to man is no less destructive in a rectory or in a suburban living room than in a courtroom or in a prison).

Powers' overt plot is, as usual, made up of simple events: some children report that a baby dove has fallen out of an inaccessibly high nest. Coerced by their "faith in themselves and the universe . . . and their faith in him" (36), the man makes futile attempts to revive the bird. He feels guilty at having sprayed the yard with DDT. Earlier that day, too, a weasel had captured a rabbit weakened by the creosote the man had placed among the lilies. He chases away a cat pursuing birds. He scolds the children for neglecting the baby dove; and, when it dies, he buries it.

Some neighbors stop to chat, but he cannot contain his emotions: "I'm sick of it all. . . . Insects, birds, and animals of all kinds. Nature. . . . That includes children. . . . *And* women. . . . And men" (41). He peremptorily refuses to serve as civil defense warden, and one of the neighbors explains to the others that the man's house is about to be torn down to make room for the college parking lot. "There's no defense against that either," he says (42). With night coming on, he goes into the house to let the bats and owls get to work.

Simple enough, the narrative is raised to the dignity of art by the elegiac style and enhanced by the carefully embedded symbols. The central figure is a man who cannot bear the pain of diminished faith, but who cannot blind himself to truth, though he tries. His initial state is simply and economically established in the opening lines: "It had been a wonderful year in the yard. . . . Until that day, there hadn't been a single casualty, *none at least that he knew about, which was the same thing*" (36). With each successive experience, the man presses more and more toward insight, until he pierces the truth, suffers pain, and makes as much adjustment to it as is possible without denying that truth. His struggle against perception begins with the identity of the baby bird:

> "Dove, isn't it?" said his wife.
>
> "I don't know," he said, afraid that he did. It was a big little bird, several shades of gray, quills plainly visible because the feathers were only beginning. . . . "A flicker maybe," he said, but he didn't think so. No, it was a dove, because where were the bird's parents? Any bird but the dove would try to do something. Somewhere in the neighborhood this baby dove's mother was posing on a branch like peace itself, with no thought of anything in her head.
>
> "Oh, God," he groaned. (36)

The dove is one of Powers' embedded symbols—embedded because it is "naturally" part of the scene; symbolic, because it carries more than a natural meaning. Why doesn't the man want the bird to be a dove? The only reason that he articulates is that "any bird but the dove would try to do something." But, as in Katherine Anne Porter's "The Grave," the dove may be taken as the Christian symbol of the Holy Spirit; of the Church, the dwelling place of the Holy Spirit; of peace and hope. Hence his groaning "Oh, God" is the beginning of awareness of the age-old Christian paradox of pain and evil in the natural world created by an all-compassionate God. (Characters in Powers' stories simply do not take the name of the Lord in vain.) But he must struggle toward theological issues.

Speculating on why the mother bird doesn't attempt to lift the baby back into the nest, he concludes that "Here was a case that showed how incompetent nature really was. . . . Nature had simply failed again" (38). But, later, he tries unsuccessfully to rationalize his way back to some faith in the natural order when he notices that the baby dove had moved:

> It had taken up its former position precisely in the center of the little raft of grass the children had made for it, and this was painful to see, this little display of order in a thing so small, so dumb, so sure. . . . He saw the bowel movement in the bottom of the dishpan as a good omen, but was puzzled by the presence of a tiny dead bug of the beetle family. It could mean that the mother had been in attendance, or it could mean that the bug had simply dropped dead from the spraying, a late casualty. (40)

In trying to cope with the mosquitoes, one of the nastier inroads of nature on human comfort, the man had sprayed the yard with DDT, and had thus joined in the cycle of killers and killed. When one of his neighbors, like Job's comforters, tries to reassure him with the usual platitudes—"There'd be too many of these doves if things like that didn't happen. . . . Look how the fish live"—the man rejects his false balm: "Mr. Hahn didn't see himself in the picture at all" (41). In January the yellow bulldozers, giant preying beasts, would come for his red house, which "in winter . . . because of the light, seemed to be bleeding" (40). And this thought leads to his bitter, hot-tempered assault on all nature and mankind:

> "That doesn't leave much, does it?" said Mr. Hahn.
>
> "No." Who was left? God. It wasn't surprising, for all problems were at bottom theological. He'd like to put a few questions to God. God, though, knowing his thoughts, knew his questions, and the world was already in possession of all the answers that would be forthcoming from God. Compassion for the Holy Family fleeing from Herod was laudable and meritorious, but it was wasted on soulless rabbits fleeing from soulless weasels. *Nevertheless, it was there just the same, or something very like it. As he'd said in the beginning, he was sick of it all.* (41)

Yet some wisdom has emerged from the heat of the experience; for, when Mr. Hahn offers to get his gun to shoot at a cat chasing a bird, the man refuses: "No. It's his nature" (41). And at this point Powers expands the range of meaning to social proportions. The man is now willing to endure the natural order of things—for animals; but he refuses to become civil defense warden, a social role which implies that man is an integral part of animal nature. Mr. Hahn, of course, does not understand: "Mr. Hahn considered him soft. He remembered that Mr. Hahn, who had an interest such as newspapers seemed to think everybody ought to have in explosions, didn't care to discuss the fall-out" (41).

Before he turns in for the night, the man sets a large stone on the dead bird's grave—"not as a marker, but as an obstacle to the cat if it returned, as he imagined it would" (42). As George Scouffas has observed, his is "not an act of sentiment, which would have reflected self-pity as well as a presumptuous assertion of self, but a gesture of opposition within his limits, a necessary moral stance."[18]

CHAPTER 3

The Fathers

IT MAY BE, as the protagonist of "Look How the Fish Live" thought, that "all problems were at bottom theological"; but in the clerical stories which have brought him fame and an identity as a Catholic writer Powers has not as a rule dealt explicitly with theological problems. Generally, these stories present such mundane matters as a nun's seeking replacement of a faulty stove in the kitchen ("The Lord's Day"), a monsignor's bullying a young curate into middle-class manners ("The Forks"), a pastor's curious relations with a termagant housekeeper ("The Valiant Woman"), a chancery official's search for the donor of an envelope addressed to the Pope ("Dawn"), a curate wangling a table from a tightwad pastor ("A Losing Game").

Powers has said that he writes "about priests for reasons of irony, comedy, and philosophy. They officially are committed to both worlds in the way most people are not. This makes for stronger beer."[1] It is easy to see that quite ordinary acts and gestures become comic or ironic when performed by a man wearing a clerical collar and a soutane: popping a knuckle in his big toe, applying Jockey Club after-shave lotion, distributing a box of divinity fudge, playing honeymoon bridge, operating a machine that separates and counts coins, evaluating a life-insurance policy. It may not be so easy to see how these acts become philosophical, but when J. F. Powers deals with them "all problems are at bottom theological."

Powers did not always approach the theological problems of the priesthood so obliquely. In fact, in his very first clerical story, "Lions, Harts, Leaping Does," Father Didymus, the aged Franciscan friar, introspectively broods about his monastic vows and his apparent lack of grace: "he had at last been placed in a position vital with meaning and precedents inescapably Christian. . . . Unsure of himself he was afraid to go on trial. It would be no minor trial . . . but one in which the greatest values were involved—a human soul and the means of its salvation or damnation" (60). The story aroused prompt and widespread admiration—it was included in both the Martha Foley and the O. Henry collections for 1944 and was reprinted in at least seven anthologies within ten years. But after this one effort Powers completely abandoned such a direct approach to the life of the spirit and, for a time, even abandoned clerical themes. When three years later he did return to a study of the priesthood in "Prince of Darkness," it was in a far more sardonic, less compassionate mood.

It is a curious fact that these first two clerical stories are at opposite ends of the spectrum—"Lions, Harts, Leaping Does" being the most tenderly elegiac, and "Prince of Darkness" the most viciously satiric. He has never gone back to the first mode (though he has approached it in the conclusion to *Morte D'Urban*), but he has created instead a succession of satiric portraits. "Lions, Harts . . ." is also unique in the Powers canon in being his only portrait of a cloistered priest.

I *"Lions, Harts, Leaping Does"*

It is rare that a young writer begins his career with so mature a work. Sister Mariella Gable has declared that "it is one of the mysteries of creative genius how a young man in his middle twenties could probe so deeply the subtle spiritual problems of an aged Franciscan."[2] With its brilliant and smoothly functioning embedded images and metaphors, its structural integrity, its profound depth of character analysis, its beautifully modulated rhythms of mood, "Lions, Harts, Leaping Does" is undoubtedly a masterpiece. Many critics still consider it Powers' finest work, and Henry Rago has described it as "one of the finest stories ever written in this country."[3]

As the story opens, in a Franciscan monastery, the pious Brother Titus reads to the aged Father Didymus from Bishop Bale's *Lives of the Popes*, after which they go for a walk in the bitter cold. Didymus meditates on his own lack of piety and regrets that his adherence to the letter of his vows prevented him from visiting his even more aged brother Seraphin, recently returned from twenty-five years in Rome. Upon re-entering the monastery, Didymus is given a telegram announcing his brother's death.

During Vespers he finds himself unable to pray, has feverish dreams, and finally collapses. Confined to a wheelchair, he is attended by Brother Titus, who presents him with a canary—"one of the Saint's own good birds" (56)—and reads to him from St. John of the Cross. Didymus suffers a dark night of the soul and, as the released canary flies out the window into the snowy arms of God, dies without finding a divine sign within himself. The action may be seen as composed of two movements—one, toward Didymus's shock of learning of his brother's death and the anguish it causes; the other, toward confronting his own death and achieving a spiritual resolution.

The central question of the story is simply expressed, but not so easily answered: does Didymus achieve salvation? All the academic critics are agreed that he does not. Ludwig and Poirier think that Didymus "knows that his awareness at death does not compensate for the failure of a lifetime. . . . The story concludes not with the glory of expiation but the heroic acceptance of its impossibility."[4] Naomi Lebowitz asserts that "In the end, Didymus does not attain saintly, satisfying peace on the verge of death."[5] To George Scouffas, ". . . ultimate deliverance he cannot achieve. . . . The story thus ends with the disconcerting vitality of love, the highest product of and antidote to human involvement and, paradoxically, the highest barrier on the passage to divinity."[6]

Without directly challenging this phalanx of critics, Brother Charles V. Padilla, a young graduate student at the University of Mexico, has squarely asserted that "Didymus actually reaches his end (to attain sanctity), but through no effort of his own. The end comes through a mysterious transformation. Sanctity is not only man's work, but God's also. The story truly reflects the contradictory ways of man and the hidden ways of God."[7] Brother Padilla is probably right.

To see that, one must first consider that the point-of-view in the story is the old priest's and that he is not necessarily the best judge of his own spiritual condition. Also, contrary to his predominant later practice, Powers' irony is not directed against his central character; rather he transforms his failings into beneficent qualities. Furthermore, there is a dynamic process of change in Didymus, from his trust in the certitude of intellect and rationality to a realization of the higher values of spirituality, and from constant self-judgment to resignation. And, finally, the implicit standard by which Didymus is ultimately to be judged shifts from the ironic denunciations of Bishop Bale (an author of "remarkable spleen") to the compassionate mysticism of St. John of the Cross.

Despite the sober, matter-of-fact tone and the solemn pace of the story, every phrase is as full of complex dissonances and nuances of meaning as the last quartets of Beethoven (which are also resolved on a note of *nunc dimittis*). For example, in the opening two paragraphs, the two old men "sat there in the late afternoon" contemplating Bishop Bale's remark that the Gospel enjoins the apostles to "stand and not sit." Anastasius "exempted from the ministry those that were lame, impotent, or diseased persons," reads Titus, whose retarded mentality moves "pathetically largo." One of the fathers "had ventured to wonder if Brother Titus, Christ preserve us, might be slightly possessed" (35). The aged Didymus is himself about to collapse in a mortal illness. "Anno 404," reads Titus, and the dates from the "funny book" are the only precise statements of time in the timeless world of the monastery. Appropriately enough, the all-pervading colors are brown and gray: "the two old men grown gray in the brown robes of the Order" sit there as the light from the wintry landscape departs the cell, leaving them "among the shadows in the room" (33).

A plaintive melodic line is struck in those opening paragraphs, and the abrupt contentiousness of Bishop Bale is diminished to a minor key by the melancholy style of the author. That opening passage shows in miniature the general movement of the story as a whole, for the crusty self-criticism of Didymus, a latter-day Bale, also gradually modulates into resignation, the *nunc dimittis* of St. John. Compare, for example, the Bishop's baleful "sooner may wine soak into any wood than any wit into those winey heads that thus both deceive themselves and slander this Godly martyr" with St. John's "birds of swift wing, lions, harts, leaping does, . . . heats and terrors that keep watch by night, by the pleasant lyres and by the siren's song, I conjure you, cease your wrath and touch not the wall" (67).[8] And compare the light imagery of the opening—"angular winter daylight forsook the small room . . . and passed through the window into the outside world"—an expiration—with that of the conclusion: "a glow . . . possessed the room slowly. Then he saw the full moon had let down a ladder of light through the window"—an inspiration.

When Didymus in the beginning is humble, he is "consciously humble"; but, in the end, his genuine humility leads him to believe that it is in Titus and not in himself that "God still chose to manifest Himself most in sanctity" (69)—the same Titus whose intellectual inferiority had amused him in the beginning when he had confronted Titus "with a distinction his simple mind could never master and which, if it could, his great soul would never recognize" (38). Perhaps the most important sign of change in Didymus is that, although at Vespers he finds himself unable to pray, he utters a "Hail Mary," just before the canary is released at the end.

It is all too easy for literary critics to become hopelessly ravelled up in tricky dialectics of theology. What are the precise conditions which determine whether a man is in a state of grace or not? In this instance one might best avoid abstract considerations simply by applying a general principle of Powers' irony: whenever a man, especially a man of the cloth, inflates himself about his own worthy qualities—as does Father Urban—he will inevitably become a target for Powers' pinprick; and whenever he genuinely laments his shortcomings and failures—as does even so despicable a breed as Father Burner—he will eventually achieve some measure of redemption.

One hesitates to reduce so complex an art as Powers' is to such a simple formula, but doing so works often enough to be useful. Besides, it is the formula which is simple, not the artistry by which the human experience is revealed. Now the crucial problem of Father Didymus—"the key and core of his trouble" (42)—which this principle can help to resolve is embodied in the dictum, "Unless a man be clearly delivered from the love of all creatures, he may not fully tend to his Creator" (42). In the beginning, Father Didymus is morally and emotionally doubled up by the fact that "as a natural man he had the desire, perhaps the inordinate desire, to see his brother again" (42), but as a friar he had refused to ask permission to go to him.

Yet he feels guilt at having "used his brother for a hair shirt" (43), and no doubt the news of his brother's death is as much responsible for his collapse as his exposure to the bitter cold. The irony is that his very anguish and suffering at having refused to go to his brother in itself absolves him from any degree of sin that may have been incurred. Indeed, had he been callously indifferent, he would have been truly unworthy. Though Didymus is a name derived from Thomas, the doubting apostle, this aged priest, no less than the Lord's disciple, proves ultimately worthy and achieves grace.

In his dream during Vespers, he sees his brother again, and their hands became "the symbol of brotherhood clasped between them" (48). But during his illness he once more flagellates himself with guilt—he "had done the right thing for the wrong reason" (59); and, again in a dream, "clearly, sensitively, he saw Seraphin and himself, just as they had always been—himself, never quite sure" (64). After he receives the last sacraments, even though in his humility he cannot possibly take upon himself the mantle of sanctity, the problem is resolved: "He wanted nothing in this world for himself at last. This may have been the first time he found his will amenable to the Divine" (65). Significant is the fact that after the last sacraments are administered to him, he does not again think of Seraphin. And now, when Titus reads to him from St. John of the Cross, Didymus is not interested even in the gentler contentiousness of the mystic: "Skip the exegesis. . . . I can do without that now. Read the verse" (67).

Yet St. John's exegesis is most appropriate to Didymus' condition; the passage that Titus is prevented from reading goes on to say: "And it is to be noted that it is not wrath and concupiscence which the Spouse conjures here, *for these faculties are never wanting in the soul,* but their troublesome and disorderly acts, which are denoted by the lions, harts, and leaping does; it is necessary in this estate that these should cease."[9] Thus, even the "Summa Angelica of mystical theology"[10] permits us to accept Didymus' desire, his concupiscence, as that which is "never wanting in the soul"; but so long as the desire "does not lead to troublesome and disorderly acts"—and Didymus did not act on that desire—it is obviously no obstacle to salvation.

Even the act itself would have been condoned by the Father Rector—"Why, Didymus, it could easily have been arranged" (46)—and had been requested by Seraphin himself (whose name is that of the highest order of angels). Finally, no less an authority than the ultimate one invoked by the story itself, St. John of the Cross, explains that the Dark Night of the Soul which leads to salvation necessarily includes exactly the kind of despair and feeling of unworthiness that Didymus experiences. St. John says, for example, that the majesty and greatness of God arouse

> "in the soul a consciousness of the other extreme which is in itself—namely, that of the deepest poverty and wretchedness: this is one of the chiefest pains that it suffers in this purgation. For it feels within itself a profound emptiness and impoverishment of three kinds of good. . . . the temporal, the natural, and the spiritual; and finds itself set in the midst of the opposite of these, namely, miseries of imperfection, aridity and emptiness of apprehensions of faculties and abandonment of the spirit in darkness. Inasmuch as God here purges the soul according to the substance of its sense and spirit, and according to the interior and exterior faculties, the soul must needs be in all his parts reduced to a state of emptiness, poverty and abandonment and must be left dry and empty and in darkness."[11]

The final irony of the story is thus charged with comic pathos. "With his whole will he tried to lose himself in the sight of God, and failed. . . . Even now he could find no divine sign within himself. He knew he had still to look outside, to Titus. God still chose to manifest himself in sanctity" (69). Hence, as Brother Padilla observes, Powers "stops short of the mystic union, but symbolically intimates it at the end in the peaceful death of Didymus."[12] The ironies are gentle, so uncharacteristic of the later Powers that even his most sympathetic critics have not noted them. For example, George Scouffas writes that "if any character in Powers' stories deserves to be called a saint, it is Titus."[13]

Now it is true that Titus at first appears to be "so delivered of the love of all creatures" that he even neglects to deliver the mail, including the telegram announcing Seraphin's death. Didymus, looking up from the telegram, "saw the grief in Titus' face. . . . It seemed to Didymus that Titus knew the meaning of the telegram. Didymus was suddenly weak, as before a miracle" (45). This rational man's readiness to accept a miracle is in itself testimony to his faith, which is also manifested in the fact that, as usual, he gives Titus more credit than he deserves. There is no "conscious humility" here!

But the Rector knows better: "Didymus, he can't forgive himself for not delivering the telegram now that he remembers it. That's all" (45). Indeed, if Titus is the standard against whom we must measure Didymus's sanctity, the aged friar comes off very well, for in the end Titus proves, within his simple-minded limits, capable of an attachment to creatures far lowlier than Father Seraphin. And the dying Didymus proves equally capable of charity and compassion when he observes it, but he refrains from his usual habit of using it as an occasion for ironic wit at Titus' expense. When the canary flies out the window into the snow, Titus

> turned stealthily to Didymus . . . fussed with the window latch and held a hand down to feel a draught, nodding anxiously as though it were the only evil abroad in the world. . . . Didymus said nothing, letting Titus keep his secret. . . . The thought of being the cause of such elaborate dissimulation in so simple a soul made Didymus want to smile—or cry, he did not know which . . . How long would it be, Didymus wondered faintly, before Titus ungrievingly gave the canary up for lost in the snowy arms of God? (69-70)

In reply to a query about the relative sanctity of the two Franciscans in "Lions, Harts . . ." Powers has said: "Yes, there is irony in Didymus's recognition of Titus's sanctity and in Didymus's failure to recognize that he has made some progress in that direction himself. Were he to recognize this, though, I would be suspicious of *it*—if he felt it were anything like 'salvation.' . . . And, yes, Didymus's spiritual condition could be superior (if you can say that) to Titus's, because of the disadvantages Didymus, as a normal person, labored under, advantages in the world's view (not, of course, that the mentally retarded necessarily have a head start on others in the pursuit of sanctity)."[14]

There are so many artistic felicities in this great story that one dare not begin to catalogue them; yet surely "Lions, Harts, Leaping Does" merits attention to details more than most fiction, and probably more than any other single short work by Powers himself. For one thing, his interpolation of patristic learning and Catholic texts seems so casually and naturally done that one might miss their particular appropriateness to the specific contexts in which they occur. For example, as the dying Didymus watches his double, the caged canary who would not sing, Titus reads from Bale that one Fabius, "as he was returning home out of the field . . . there was a pigeon seen standing on his head and suddenly he was created pastor of the Church, which he looked not for" (57)—as Didymus himself looked not for salvation. Then, as Titus reads of Pope Marcellus, who is confined by the Emperor to a stable and "daily tormented with strife and noisomeness" (63), Didymus interrupts Titus because the canary suddenly raises a fuss in attempting to escape from its cage. Thus the early martyr-popes, the canary, and Didymus are established as a set of correspondences since each seeks the snowy arms of God. Didymus, too, is "one of the Saint's own good birds."

Early in the story, Didymus is still the hard-headed rationalist ready, like Bale, to lash out against "the dunderheads and fools" (38) who through the ages had perverted theology and the humanities. But the coils of his own logic trammel him as he meditates on the fact that his "abecedarian observance of the vows did not promise perfection" (42). Poverty? He was penniless, but quite well-off compared with "one-third of the nation" (40). Chastity? A dead issue for an old man. Obedience? No longer difficult, now that he was conditioned. No, the one self-denial that had cost Didymus a painful effort and which established his integrity as a friar he diminishes with logic-chopping.

Throughout the story, beautifully effective images and symbols mark significant events: feeling "saved" because it is merely Titus who catches him asleep at Vespers, he rises only to sink back to the floor, which "with fingers smelling of dust and genesis, reached up and held him. . . . For a radiant instant . . . he saw the justice of his position" (52). When Titus first leaves the concealed bird-cage in his room, Didymus congratulates himself for suppressing the sin of curiosity; but "a moment later the keystone of his good intention crumbled, and the whole edifice of detachment with it. . . . Didymus moved his hands to the wheels of his chair."

Especially effective is the functional use of landscape images, which not only reflect Didymus's shifting visual acuity during his illness, but also embody cosmic significance: ". . . fearful the gentle boughs under scrutiny would turn into hideous, waving tentacles, he looked. . . . Gauzily rain descended in a fine spray, hanging in fat berries from the wet black branches . . . cold, crystal drops. . . . Watching the raindrops prove gravity, he was grateful for nature's, rather than his, return to reason" (54).

If there is anything to regret in the subsequent development of Powers' narrative artistry, it is not that he has perfected the colloquial idiom as his chief narrative vehicle, but that he has largely abandoned the marvelous lyric gift manifested in his first great story. Of course, in the later stories, Powers never is at loss for a striking metaphor, and he often shows compassion for his characters; but after "Lions, Harts . . ." he never again attempts such delicate tenderness of mood and language.

This poetry reaches a height in the dream of Father Didymus, a dream which, brief as it is, gives the impression of real problems being encountered in a strange, unreal world. Even if, unlike the intricate dream passages of Joyce, every detail is not subject to precise explication, the dream is in broad terms meaningful and not merely a vague, bizarre phenomenon. Seeking light from the outside—from a room across the court or from the moon—Didymus sees only the red sanctuary light. Unable to pray, he falls into meditation and into a dream in which he achieves a wish-fulfillment and a foreshadowing—his meeting with his brother Seraphin. If the reunion occurs within a spiralling brown coil of a serpent river, that signifies that Didymus, in his guilt at having transgressed the spirit of his vows while observing the letter, feels he may be swallowed by the devil. But both he and Seraphin remain unafraid and clasp their hands in brotherhood—they are immune to any terrors.

The river then becomes Jonah's whale, but the brothers feel only a mock distress and look calmly on an occasional large fish and a mass of seething crustacea. They talk of ordinary things such as death—the death of their parents and of themselves: "The sound of dirt descending six feet to clatter on the coffins was memorable but unmentionable" (49). Then, in the most casual manner and without the slightest trace of rivalry, they talk of their life's work: Seraphin's slow and patient labors in Rome to get a saint canonized; Didymus pounding away at teaching geometry, "giving Pythagoras no rest in his grave" (49). But a black crayfish seizes Didymus at his knees and back. Seraphin, safely dead, may remain in that strange dream world, but Didymus—whose problems cannot be solved by wishful dreams—is summoned back to painful reality, to the agonies of his mind and body. And, as he rises to consciousness, "the sun like molten gold squirted him in the eye"—just as Plato said it always does. Blinded by reality, his consciousness spreads "like ink in a blotter" (50); and he asks Titus, who is rousing him, to put out the candle. He must still experience the dark night of the soul before he can, like the canary, lose himself in the snowy arms of God.

II *"Prince of Darkness"*

"Lions, Harts, Leaping Does" portrays a lean and saintly cloistered friar, whose only desire is to be worthy of God's approval but whose anguish comes from his testing himself so severely that on his deathbed he finds himself unworthy. "Prince of Darkness" portrays a totally different kind of priest moving in exactly the opposite direction. With derisive irony, the story depicts a fat, boorish, incompetent curate, Father Burner, whose fervent desire is to find a secure niche as a pastor and eventually to retire to a comfortable old age. More aptly than any two other Powers stories, it might be said that "Lions, Harts . . ." is "grace-centered" and that "Prince of Darkness" is "gravity-centered."[15] But each is, in its way, a masterpiece.

"Prince of Darkness" takes us on a different kind of "long day's journey into night." The story begins with Father Burner, twenty years out of the seminary and still a curate, making friends at breakfast with the Mammon of Iniquity. Offered "security" in the form of an old-age annuity by one Thomas Nash Tracy ("T.N.T."), he feels he "must not reject the olive branch because it came by buzzard" (221). When two young seminary graduates, Fathers Quinlan and Keefe, join him at breakfast, Burner operates "on the principle of discord at any cost" in vicious verbal duels about the state of the clergy, the parish, and the world (226). Later, alone in his room, Burner practices putting a golf ball into his clerical collar and has fantasies about being a "par-shattering padre," a German war ace.

After writing another letter to the Archbishop requesting a transfer (in the hope of getting a parish of his own), he drives to the airport to put in some flying time toward his pilot's license; but the rain keeps him grounded. (Father Burner will not soar that day.) After a hearty lunch at a hamburger joint, he goes to the hospital to visit his old friend, Father Desmond, who is being treated for alcoholism. Upon his return to the Deanery, Father Burner is informed that the Chancery wants him to hear confessions that night—the usual way of being summoned for a conference with the Archbishop. After a series of confessions in which he mercilessly bullies the would-be penitents, he is ushered in the presence of the Archbishop, who—despite Burner's obsequious manner, or rather, because of it—obliquely instructs Burner in piety and simply transfers him as curate to another parish.

The events alone reveal the thoroughly secular outlook of Father Burner, but the most brilliant revelations of the fat priest's immersion in gluttonous fleshliness are in the rapier-thrusts of dialogue, accompanied by the unconscious but eloquent gestures; the wish-fulfillment reveries juxtaposed with abrasive realities; and the subtleties of imagery and metaphor in the descriptions—all pervaded with such astringent irony that the delineation is cruel.

Though "Prince of Darkness" is over thirteen thousand words long, the longest story published by Powers in the first twenty years of his career, it hangs on one of the most tenuous plot lines. The central question is first suggested by Tracy in the breakfast scene: "I guess security's one thing we're all after" (216). The rest is revelation of the various schemes and dreams by which Father Burner hopes to achieve security in the highest terms available to him—a parish of his own—until he reaches the climax in which his hopes are frustrated. Even more than in "Lions, Harts . . ." characterization is of greater importance than action, but Powers shrewdly stretches out the revelation of character because clearly seeing Father Burner in the beginning would give away the whole show. For example, to describe the body of so committed a materialist is to describe his soul; and Powers cannily delays and extends that description as long as he dares.

Gradually the details accumulate: at breakfast "Father Burner's sausage fingers . . . . worked up sweat in the folds of the napkin" (215). The two newly ordained priests "were hardly inside the dining room before he was explaining how he came to be eating breakfast so late—so late, see—not *still*! 'You protest too much, Father,' Quinlan said. 'The Angelic Doctor himself weighed three hundred pounds, and I'll wager he didn't get it all from prayer and fasting.' " Shaking hands with the Deanery guest, he "experienced the fat man's contempt and envy for the thin man" (223). Irritated by Quinlan's teasing, "Father Burner grimaced, the flesh rising in sweet, concentric tiers around his mouth" (230). While dressing for his trip to the airport, "reluctantly he pulled on his black trousers, falling across the bed to do so, . . . legs heaving up like howitzers. . . . He stood looking down at the buckle, chins kneading softly with the effort" (242). During the drive, he "plunged his hams deeper into the cushions, tugged viciously at both knees, loosening the binding black cloth, easing the seat" (245).

A knowledge of his appearance increases the hilarity of the epithet directed at the "circular priest" after an article of his appeared with the misprint for "secular." But the sinister implications of his obesity are strikingly expressed in the description of Father Burner in the confession box: "A big spider drowsy in his web, drugged with heat and sins, he sat waiting for the next one to be hurled into his presence by guilt ruddy ripe." The furniture of his mind reveals him to be a most unworthy priest indeed. Apart from his urge to use the Church as a means to the easy life and as an arena for the exercise of petty power, he is marked by deficiencies of mind and spirit that would be reprehensible in any man even outside the priesthood.

His personal relations are all charged with strife and tension, for Father Burner either lords it over his inferiors or grovels before his superiors. His only friend is Father Desmond, an alcoholic, whom he denies to the Archbishop. He deals with most men in terms of stereotypes, usually ethnic: "why is it the Irish without exception are always laying personal claim to church property?" (226). He believes that it is "certainly to be expected in any Latin country" (234) that the men will not attend church. Even his conception of himself is in such terms: "He had a light heart for a German American of German descent" (263). Moreover, his cultural values are atrocious: "Francis Thompson was the only Limey worth his salt . . . you can have your Hopkins. . . . Include me out, as Sam Goldwyn says" (229). He admires the cleverness of advertising phrases and has no taste for music.

Taken by themselves, these unfortunate characteristics would serve merely to show Father Burner as a sad specimen of humanity. But the gestures of his mind and body are figured forth in images and metaphors that darken the chiaroscuro; they reveal him as almost the satanic figure which both his surname and his nickname, "The Prince of Darkness," suggest. As an emissary of the devil, he actually despises the earth and those who would save mankind. Burner breakfasts in a room which "reproduced the world, all wonders and horrors. . . . The world globes simpered in the shadows, heavy-headed idiot boys, listening . . . heard everything and understood nothing" (216-17). And this description is immediately followed by the suggestive gesture, "Father Burner put his big black shoe on a moth and sent dust flecks crowding up a shaft of sunlight to the distant ceiling" (217).

When Father Keefe congratulates Father Burner on the beautiful church he has at St. Patrick's, he responds, "'*I* have? . . . *Me*?'" He jabbed at the grapefruit before him, his second, demolishing its perfect rose window" (226). So much is packed into that passage—much that is so meaningful on the strictly realistic level that one might easily miss the farthest overtones. Of course, it is his second grapefruit. Of course, he is chafing at the fact that he hasn't a church of his own, that he is out of place in an Irish-dominated parish, a St. Patrick's which he resents so much he could smash it. (He later drops a match in the holy-water font.) Both his personality and his situation are illuminated in a flash of language. It is not necessary to convert the real-life drama into allegory to see here and elsewhere the satanic quality of Father Burner. He draws the shade against the sun; he speaks with a mouthful of smoke; he constantly burns with earnest resentment. In his car he exhales a cloud of smoke which "whirled about the little St. Christopher garroted from the ceiling" (245) and applies "a cloven hoof to the pedal" (254). (Only in the presence of the Archbishop does he decline to smoke.) While visiting Father Desmond, he sits "deep in a red leather chair" (256), having been unable to "go up" in his airplane.

Such details may not carry a full weight of satanic meaning by themselves, but they reinforce the impressions created by Burner's total lack of religious spirit. However much Powers may lampoon the super-pious jellyfish who inhabit so many of his rectories, his greatest contempt is for those petty Fascists of the parishes who live benighted lives in actual contempt of the spirit of the Church, but who are ever ready to apply its rules rigidly whenever someone may be hurt by them. Father Burner regards as a "nice account" a parish family that contributes regularly to the Church. In his opinion the best counteraction to the Depression is a Perpetual Novena—and to the war ("a terrible thing") a victory altar. It is no wonder that this fat materialist chose for his ordination gift a watch (commitment to this world's time) rather than the usual chalice. He is not adept at praying and fasting, and he is utterly unable to plan a sermon. He doesn't read his Office, and he is a devil in the confession box. All his deficiencies in his interview with the Archbishop, who slyly points out that there are no saints named Ernest and who elicits from Burner the admission that he hasn't read St. Bernard lately (and we are reminded of Father Didymus's self-laceration in recalling Bernard's dictum that "Hell is paved with the bald pates of priests!") (68).

The meaning that gathers force throughout the story is explicitly stated in the end by the Archbishop, whom Powers has affirmed to be the "norm against which the deviation of the main character can be measured":[16] "Today there are few saints, fewer sinners, and everybody is already saved. We are all heroes in search of an underdog. As for villains, the classic kind with no illusions about themselves, they are . . . extinct. The very devil, for instance—where the devil is the devil today, Father?. . . . It is rather to the center, I think we should look—to ourselves, the devil in us" (273-74). There is a devil in Burner. Yet he is a man and a priest, not a puppet representing

Evil in a morality play. Hence, he has a complex character in whom there are some graces, even if they are not "saving" graces.

He is, for example, "slightly repelled" at Tracy's description of the retirement annuity as "heavenly life insurance" (217) and recognizes the man to be a buzzard. When a mother complains that no star was put on the church flag for her drafted son, Burner "was sorry for her" (237). He is touched by a little boy's desire to "be a priest like you, Father" (246); and for a moment he feels certain that, "yes, if he had to, he would die for the Faith" (247). But in a painful self-analysis, he recognizes that were he to become a chaplain and meet death while carrying the Holy Eucharist to a dying soldier, that "would be only exterior justification for him, a last bed for public approbation, a short cut to nothing" (250). He is embarrassed by the memory of a child being reluctant in his presence to name *gluttony* as one of the seven deadly sins. Like the damned souls in the first circle of Dante's Inferno, he knows what virtue is and knows that he has it not:

> The mark of the true priest was heavy on the Dean. The mark was on Quinlan; it was on Keefe. It was on every priest he could think of, including a few on the bum, and his good friend and bad companion, Father Desmond. But it was not on him, not properly. They, the others, were stained with it beyond all disguise or disfigurement—indelibly, as indeed Holy Orders by its sacramental nature must stain, for keeps in this world and the one to come. "Thou art a priest forever." With him, however, it was something else and less, a mask or badge which he could and did remove at will, a temporal part to be played. . . . (253-54)

Even so, one must remember that, when Milton's Satan found his own vile condition loathesome, he was no less satanic. Father Burner, the man who "could scarcely see the cross glowing on the dome" (277) of the Cathedral, gets his comeuppance in the end—and from a godly man who is, within Powers' more modest dimensions, no less triumphant and no less vindictive than Milton's God: "You will report on August 8 to the Reverend Michael Furlong, to begin your duties on that day as his assistant. I trust that in your new appointment you will find not peace but a sword" (277).

III *Other Father Burner Stories*

If the subsequent stories about Father Burner may be taken as sequels to "Prince of Darkness"—and there are difficulties in doing so—then one must conclude that he truly had saving graces within him. The use of a character in more than one story can serve the valuable purpose of enabling an author to explore more fully the complexity of that character or the particular milieu in which he functions. But if there is to be an artistic unity among the several stories, there must be no radical, unexplained shift of personality and the narrative tone and techniques must be of the same order (as in Katherine Anne Porter's Miranda stories). The Father Burner of "Death of a Favorite" and "Defection of a Favorite" is, admittedly, also a fat priest befriended by fellow priests addicted to drink, cars, and baseball, and desperate for a parish of his own. But in these stories he does *not* "operate on the principle of discord at any cost." On the contrary, he is goaded by others into foolish and petty acts that never reach serious proportions. Powers' wit is whimsical, not vicious, and the final tone is of domestic rather than cosmic comedy. Burner no longer smokes—or burns. He has mellowed considerably.

These changes in character are concomitants of a change in narrative point-of-view from Burner to the rectory cat, Fritz. The psycho-moral intensity and the irony that derives from the introspections of a secularly, perhaps even satanically, oriented priest are no longer possible; and—unfortunately—the cat's introspections do not serve as an adequate substitute. Yet the most enthusiastic reviewer of *The Presence of Grace* considers "Defection of a Favorite" to be the best story in the collection and praises Fritz as "something of a combination of Saki's burlesque talking cat and one of Kafka's talking animals."[17] And another critic says that Fritz is "surely one of the best realized cats in all literature."[18] But Evelyn Waugh, who knows better, says "it is not enough to portray the personality of a sharp child and endow it with a few extraneous attributes of brute creation. . . . The essence of the observing and recording animal should be false conclusion, the irony established by the reader's knowledge of what the humans are really up to and the cat's erroneous explanations based upon cat's motives."[19]

Although neither Waugh nor anyone else can possible lay down a binding *a priori* law governing any writer's choice of perspective, it nevertheless is true that any first-person narrative immediately raises a problem of balance and focus. Unfortunately in Powers' cat stories there is a lack of balance and a constant shifting of focus between the point of view of the narrative medium, Fritz, and the chief object of his attention, Father Burner. Hence, the cat stories are badly flawed in technique and lack sufficient ironic tension. In "Death of a Favorite" when the cat, whom Father Malt introduces to his guests as "my assistant," confesses his belief that "it is naked power that counts most in any rectory" (25); observes that his presence "brought out the beast in them [the priests]—which is to say very nearly all that was in them" (43); or when, in the companion story, he protests against Father Burner's "fouling his own nest wherever he went, upstairs or down" (109); notices certain "lapses or inconsistencies in Father Burner" (112)—all these serve as an amusing revelation of the similarity between the cat and Father Burner. As Fritz himself observes, "the ironic part was that Father Burner and I . . . had a lot in common" (109).

But there are long stretches in these stories where the necessary relation of medium and narrative is broken and where each segment bears an interest entirely its own, as when Fritz is forced to become a mouser or when he unobtrusively presents long sequences of dialogue among the priests. Even though Fritz may be seen as Burner's alter ego—and he is a priest of a cat with his black fur and white collar, his self-imposed celibacy, and his status as Father Malt's "assistant"—he remains both too much and not enough of a feline to bear the role successfully.

Furthermore, as a character study of the "circular priest," these stories are severely flawed by the inaccessibility of Father Burner's motives for his deeds. What can be known or inferred about his motives simply does not fit "the prince of darkness" depicted in the earlier story. He is still obsessed with automobiles and sports, still neglectful of his parish duties, still in the grip of sloth, envy, and gluttony, and still a knocker (he says of Father Malt's housekeeper, who serves an inedible bread pudding, "Sometimes I think he got her from a hospital and sometimes . . . I think she came from one of *your* fine institutions."). But there is no imagery of fire and smoke or the cloven hoof;

there is no manifestation of the self-loathing accompanying an intense longing to become a pastor; and there is no abrasive sadism in his dealing with others.[20] Curiously, he has suddenly become a shrewd judge of literature, one able to say of Arthur Koestler: "a writer who's ahead of his time—about fifteen minutes. Good on jails and concentration camps" (27). He is perhaps more tolerant and has more of the ecumenical spirit: "I like 'em [the Masons] better than K.C.'s. . . . Gazing off in the direction of the Mason's big house, he said 'I've played golf with him!'" (29).

The new Father Burner of the cat stories is never the source of evil. There is always someone like Father Philbert, the nut, or Father Desmond, the not-quite-reformed alcoholic, to initiate unpriestly behavior. In "Death of a Favorite," Philbert suggests starving Fritz into becoming a mouser, and he blasphemously seizes the crucifix off the wall and pushes Fritz's face into it to induce a conditioned evasive response that will lead Father Malt, the exorcist, to believe that the cat is possessed. And, interestingly, it is Father Burner who demurs: "Sure it's all right to go on with this thing?" (43). The trick works and the fleeing cat is killed by the clerical-gray Olds driven by the rookie priest. But, being a cat, Fritz is immediately reborn to enter the rectory and cause Burner to be sent back to his usual place at the foot of the table.

"Defection of a Favorite" is not so whimsical a story, but the serious issue of Father Burner's spiritual regeneration is almost reduced to levity by Powers' continued use of the cat's point of view. Suddenly thrust into a position of responsibility when the aged Father Malt is hospitalized after a fall, Father Burner now carefully removes his galoshes before entering the rectory, turns out lights where they are not needed, buys the housekeeper a kitchen radio, spends hours on sick calls and preparation of sermons, wins more converts than Malt ever did, and studies volumes of *Church Property Administration.* "It almost seemed as if he were out to distinguish himself, not in the eyes of others . . . but in his own eyes" (114). And curiously, his new-found vocation leads to a friendly attitude toward the cat, who responds in kind, even though he cannot bring himself to eat the baby mice caught in Burner's trap. And Fritz is pleased when, in response to Father Desmond's query "Does he ever bring you a mouse?," Burner covers up for him with an evasion, "You don't see any around, do you?" (126).

It is Desmond who does all the prodding and politicking to get Burner a parish of his own, and it is also Desmond who almost ruins Burner's chances by arranging a drinking and poker-playing party at the rectory on the very evening that the Archbishop drops in. On that occasion, Father Burner is "saved" by Fritz:

> "Do you like animals, Father? . . . This one, I see, likes you," said the Archbishop, smiling. "Some believe it to be an infallible sign, the best of character references."
>
> Father Burner blushed and said, "I wish I could believe in that sign, your Excellency."
>
> I trotted over to the Archbishop, selected his black trouser leg from all the others, and brushed against it, nicely purring. Everyone laughed.
>
> "Credo!" cried Father Burner. (120-21)

Nevertheless, even though Burner does a "bang-up job" for more than fourteen months, the Archbishop is powerless to force Father Malt to retire against his will. And one evening while Desmond is foolishly gossiping to Burner about his chances of taking over the parish, Father Malt suddenly appears on crutches and Desmond flees:

> They stared at each other, Father Malt and Father Burner, like two popes themselves not sure which one was real. . . . I turned my back on Father Burner, went over to Father Malt, and favored him with a solemn purr. . . . As long as he lived, he had to be a pastor, I saw; his need was the greater. And Father Burner, saw it too. He went up to Father Malt, laid a strong, obedient hand on the old one that held tight to the right crutch, and was then the man he was becoming.
>
> "Hello, boss," he said. "Glad you're back."
>
> It was his finest hour. In the past, he had lacked the will to accept setbacks with grace and had derived no merit from them. It was difficult to believe that he'd profited so much from my efforts in his behalf—my good company and constant example. I was happy for him. (128-29)

The problem is not that a man like Burner could not possibly rise to the occasion but that some credible manifestation of spiritual motivation, some explanation of how it is possible, is required. What is suggested in "Defection of a Favorite" is that Burner all along needed not the office and the security of being pastor but rather the confidence of knowing that he had the ability. Having proved that to himself, he can face anything. But the psycho-moral metamorphosis of Father Burner in the cat stories is not satisfactorily dramatized; it is merely asserted—which makes the cat stories unworthy sequels to such a magnificent story as "Prince of Darkness."

Powers has proved himself in his short stories a master of character revelation, but he is not very successful at depicting the process of character change. Possibly his deficiency in this respect has something to do with the nature of the short-story form, for in the limited dimensions of that genre only two kinds of characterization are readily possible—the gradual revelation of a personality through a series of "ordinary" experiences, as in "Prince of Darkness"; or the dramatic change of a character through crisis, through the confrontation of some traumatic experience, as in "Lions, Harts, Leaping Does." The *gradual* change of a character as he meets the more or less regular demands of everyday life seems to require the larger scope of the novel.

But the sudden change of a character as he goes about his usual round cannot be credible in any genre. Since Powers very early abandoned stories of violence, he was almost automatically committed to writing studies in character revelation—such as "The Valiant Woman," "The Lord's Day," and "The Forks"; and these have been most successful when the point of view has been the introspective one of the central character. Such is the case in "Prince of Darkness" and in "The Valiant Woman," two stories which Powers himself considers the best of his first collection.

IV *"The Valiant Woman"*

Typically, the introspective technique allows for the kind of irony and ambiguity that can suggest profound depths with a great economy of means. "The Valiant Woman" is a perfect example, a story that can easily be misread as simply a great joke on the clergy—and a hilarious joke it is. Poor Father Firman, a priest, finds himself trapped in an unbreakable union with a termagant housekeeper whose meddlesome ways and unrestrained tongue have driven away all his friends. The story presents Father

Firman's fifty-ninth birthday party, a pathetic affair attended only by Father Firman's last friend, Father Frank Nulty—and he is soon routed by Mrs. Stoner's intrusive inanities. As soon as he is gone, Mrs. Stoner seizes the opportunity for one of their regular games of honeymoon bridge. As usual, she plays for blood; and as usual Father Firman loses miserably, for his mind is occupied—he is brooding on the impossibility of getting rid of her. While preparing for bed, Father Firman lunges at a mosquito, misses, but breaks a statue of St. Joseph. From the hallway, Mrs. Stoner berates him: "Shame on you, Father. She needs the blood for her eggs" (175).

"The Valiant Woman" has three movements: an opening dialogue during the birthday dinner, which dramatically establishes the sad plight of Father Firman; his interior monologue during the bridge, which develops his internal struggle to the point of climax; and a hilarious, pathetic final action, in which Father Firman is symbolically defeated. But there is no shifting in point of view; Father Firman remains the central intelligence throughout. And though he is chiefly preoccupied with his awful housekeeper, his meditations and mannerisms reveal the nature of his own soul.

The title of the story, as Winifred Lynskey was the first to observe, is taken from Proverbs and points up one of the crucial ironies:[21]

> Who shall find a valiant woman? . . . The heart of her husband trusteth in her: and he shall have no need of spoils. She will render him good, and not evil, all the days of her life. . . . She hath girded her loins with strength, and hath strengthened her arm. She hath tasted and seen that her traffic is good: her lamp shall not be put out in the night. . . . Her husband is honourable in the gates when he sitteth among the senators of the land. . . . he hath opened her mouth to wisdom: and the law of clemency is on her tongue.[22]

Now some of these lines are bitterly true of Mrs. Stoner; others are woeful reversals of the situation in the story. All in all, they make the narrative a parody of domestic life. And as Robert Penn Warren observes, the whole situation is presented in the opening page: Mrs. Stoner's domination of the conversation; her churchiness, which we know does not have a shred of real piety in it but merely a kind of gossipy clubbiness; her scatterbrained irrelevancies which move easily from soybeans to converts; Father Nulty's strained politeness to his friend's housekeeper; Father Firman's yawn. "It all comes over directly in a flash, without discussion or preparation."[23]

Father Firman is not very firm when Mrs. Stoner stones him: "And cut your toenails, why don't you? Haven't I got enough to do?" (167). This situation is very much like the one Father Burner in "Prince of Darkness" was resolved to avoid if he got a parish with his mother as housekeeper: "It would not be the old story of the priest taking orders from his housekeeper, even if she was his mother (seminarians, from winter evenings of shooting the bull, knew only too well the pitfalls of parish life)" (264). Yet there is a deeper dimension to the story than the irony of a parish housekeeper oblivious of the gulf that lies between her and the man in Holy Orders whose dignity she destroys. As she cracks the whip over the cards and tames them into a neat deck, Father Firman declines to cut and, knowing she would prefer it, invites her to play first. Is he thus revealing how utterly crushed he is in her presence (which would make this one of Powers' hard-irony stories), or is he manifesting a kind of saintly patience? (This would suggest that "The Valiant Woman" is a kind of clerical companion piece to "The Poor Thing.")

The issue is not easy to resolve, for every bit of evidence seems to be qualified by other indications. For example, Father Firman's introspection throughout the card game is made up of a sequence of mutually cancelling thoughts: like the mosquito, "she played for blood . . . [but] he found her ferocity pardonable, more a defect of the flesh, venial, while his own trouble was all in the will, mortal" (168). More important than the accuracy of his interpretation of Mrs. Stoner's defects is his judgment of his own, and this middle section modulates the story into a study of the priest's own soul. The more he tries to be patient and understanding, the more frustrated he becomes and the more he reveals his own crucial failings: surely she hadn't cheated in playing her last trump—"she believed in being fair. Besides he had been watching her" (168). There was at least one other priest worse off with a housekeeper, but Cronin "was quite a freak himself" (169). Unable to muster a genuine trace of

Christian charity, he comes to the "heart of the matter, the essence. The essence was that housekeepers were hard to get— . . . yes, harder to get than assistants or vocations" (170).

The story might have concluded with the game of honeymoon bridge, "the bitter end of their long day together. . . . She made her way up the stairs, carrying the tea, followed by the cat, purring" (171-72). But that ending would have achieved closure without a thorough exploration of the irony of the title and would have left undeveloped the powerful mosquito symbolism. Again Powers turns the screw another thread. In the final section of the story, Father Firman recalls how in the earliest days of her service at the rectory (during "the honeymoon") Mrs. Stoner had won use of the guest room by complaining of the mosquitoes in the back room—and how that had put a stop to overnight visits from his friends. Even the gentle Father Nulty had taken to humming "Wedding Bells Are Breaking Up That Old Gang of Mine," before he saw how serious the situation was and took pity. For some time now Father Firman had been studying the regulations governing a priest's residence with a woman (seeking grounds for divorce). And again, his charitable rationalization that "it would be a slimy way of handling it after all her years of service" is undercut by a more selfish and worldly consideration: "He could not afford to pension her off, either" (174).

Perhaps Powers intends only to show a befuddled old man whose weakness of will, since he is a priest in Holy Orders, amounts to a serious moral failing. Wittingly or not, however, Powers accumulates details that add up to a psychological as well as a moral situation. Mrs. Stoner is certainly obsessed with the idea of marriage: prying into baptismal and matrimonial records in the hope of "uncover[ing] a bastard and flush[ing] him out of the rectory"; holding her nose over bad marriages in the presence of the victims; berating bewildered couples for entering into mixed marriages merely "to give the child a name." After coming to the rectory, she hadn't even tried for a husband and had told Father Firman that she had "given him the best years of her life" (170). Though not the valiant woman of Proverbs, she is as much a wife as she wants to be—which is precisely the insight which Father Firman approaches and vehemently rejects: "Had she got her wires crossed and mistaken him all these years for *that*? *That*! Him! Suffering God! No. That was getting morbid. No. He must not think of that again, ever. No" (173).

However, the final irony is that Father Firman is as much a husband as he wants to be! Else why does he construe the situation in terms of impossible alternatives—either get rid of her entirely or submit to her wifely domination? Thus, Firman's weakness is not merely a failure of will; it is the manifestation of another, subconscious will: Father Firman suffers the fate of a hen-pecked husband because he wants to. His fury at the mosquito which bites him on the back is, of course, fury at Mrs. Stoner; but, less obviously and more significantly, he is angry with himself. He is no St. Joseph divinely guided in a relationship with a woman who cannot properly be his wife—nor is she anything remotely resembling the Mother of the Church. In lunging at the mosquito, Father Firman smashes the statue of St. Joseph to the floor; and in one of the most brilliant satiric strokes in all his fiction, Powers concludes the story with satanic powers:

> "What is it, Father? Are you hurt?"
> "Mosquitoes—damn it! And only the female bites!"
> Mrs. Stoner, after a moment, said, "Shame on you, Father. She needs the blood for her eggs. . . ."
> He lunged again. (175)

Thus Powers turns "The Valiant Woman" into an implacable character revelation of a priest, who, if not a prince, is at least a slave of darkness. This story is one of Powers' finest performances; and although it is widely reprinted as a humorous study of rectory life, it better deserves a place in Powers' portrait gallery of unworthy priests.

Each of Powers' first three stories dealing with the motif of the unworthy priest—"Lions, Harts, Leaping Does," "Prince of Darkness," and "The Valiant Woman"—maintains the point of view of the priest himself. But as we move from one story to the next, there is a gradual diminishing of the extent to which the priest's insight is shown to be redeeming. Didymus judges himself unworthy of sanctity and is thereby saved; Burner faces his corruption as a priest only to remain corrupt; and Firman recoils from looking at the truth and is thereby damned. Curiously, the acerbic wit increases, as if the greatest horror most needed the protective covering of comedy.

V *"The Lord's Day"*

In his next story of rectory life, "The Lord's Day," Powers presents another unworthy priest, "a fat vision in black" (1)—an anti-intellectual, penny-pinching lout who guzzles beer and listens to the radio (switching from the symphony and the Catholic Hour to baseball and a war drama), while the sisters count the Sunday collections. But this priest is not the center of attention; the point of view is that of the harrassed Mother Superior, and the central problems of the story are hers: how to fulfill her responsibilities to her sisters by securing the interest and cooperation of the pastor, and how to control her wrath and preserve both decorum and Christian charity when he refuses.

The shortest of all Powers' collected stories, "The Lord's Day" is by no means the simplest; for in less than three thousand words he has performed an astounding feat. He has captured the diverse personalities of several nuns, a priest and his curate, and a Mother Superior (whose psyche is thoroughly explored).

The action all occurs on the Lord's Day. As usual, there are three movements to the story: first, there is a one-paragraph opening exposition, in which the Mother Superior recalls unsuccessfully pleading with the "incredible priest" to spare the trees which provide shade for the school playground. He had ordered them cut down as the only means of getting rid of some bees which had stung him. "What if it had been a wasp? How did he know it was one of the mulberry bees? He knew. That was all. And now, Sister, if you'll just take the others into the house with you, we'll get down to work" (1). Thus, in a few deft strokes, Powers sketches the stupidity, obstinacy, officiousness, and hypocrisy of a man who is aroused only when he can cut something—or somebody—down. And since this is presented from the point of view of the Sister, Powers shows that she is aware of those qualities in him, yet persists in trying to salvage something—and temporarily succeeds: "The three big ones must go. He would spare the small one until such time as it grew up and became a menace" (1).

After the initial exposition, Powers shows in the second part of the story the delicate sensibilities and hardheaded common sense of this remarkable woman as she rounds up the nuns to count the offerings:

> They were waiting in the parlor. She knew at a glance that one was missing. Besides herself, they were twelve—the apostles. It was the kind of joke they could appreciate, but not to be carried too far, for then one of them must be Judas, which was not funny. In the same way she, as the leader of the apostles, feared the implication as blasphemous. It was not a very good joke for the convent, but it was fine to tell lay people, to let them know there was life there. (1-2)

As the nuns reluctantly file into the counting room to begin their sordid labors, Powers presents brilliant little pen portraits: Sister Antonia, whose appointment as assistant is a tribute to the Mother Superior's skill, generates action—while mocking the value of it—with her cry, "Come on, you money-changers, dig in . . . Money, money, money" (3). Sister Florence, a timid little yes-woman, shy, not very bright, eager to help, finds the going easier if converted into a game and obliquely suggests it: "Shall we do what we did last week?" (4). The two old-timers, Sister Louise and Sister Paula, who cannot forget that Sunday had been a day of rest in the old dispensation, expressed their resentment in varying ways—the first dozes off, and the second (known as Sister Cigar Box among the students) grumbles and makes wisecracks, referring to Father O'Hannon of St. Jude's as "Father O'Mammon . . . of St. Judas's" (5). Sister Eleanor, quiet and cooperative, makes whatever adjustments are necessary; it is she who, unable to get an appropriation from the pastor for a school map of the United States, is assembling one from road maps sent by various oil companies.

Thus, while women committed to the spiritual life count and tabulate sacks of money, the whole quality and atmosphere of parish life are vividly realized. It is clearly one in which anything useful will have to be accomplished by the nuns' rebelling against or outwitting the priest; and no help will come from the young curate, a heavy athlete, who grandly drives away to play golf after excusing himself from the evening devotions.

The implications of speeches and gestures are beautifully augmented by wry innuendoes in the imagery of the story. From her window the Mother Superior watches the priest go to give the first lick of the axe to the trees: "Waves of heat wandered thirstily over the pebbles, led around by the uncertain wind. She could see the figure of Father walking the heat waves." Far from being a Christ-figure, the satanic priest walks in his own inferno. The destruction of the trees makes the schoolground a wasteland: "Going under the basketball standards she thought they needed only a raven or two to become gibbets in the burning sun" (2). Though the priest has modernized his kitchen, he is still prey to corruption: "A cockroach turned around and ran the other way on the sink" (3). The satanic figure tempts the nuns: "'Like apples? Who wants an apple?' . . . He placed the bowl on the table for them. Three apples on top were real, but the ones underneath were wax and appeared more edible. No one took an apple" (8). Thus Powers charges the realistic events with overtones of meaning.

In the last two pages the action builds to the third movement, a wryly ironic climax. As the pastor rests in an orange-and-green deck chair, the Mother Superior asks him to examine the ancient, irreparable stove in the nunnery (needless to say, the rectory kitchen is gleamingly modern). "Today? *Now*?" he replies, implying that surely she must realize that Sunday is the Lord's Day. However, the Mother Superior has timed her request with the precision of an experienced strategist, for, the nuns have of course spent the Lord's Day doing the priest's dirty work. On his way to the nunnery, "he scooped his collar off the radio and let it snap around his neck. He left it that way, unfastened" (10). Of the obsolete monstrosity in the kitchen he says, "They don't make them like that anymore" (11) and then attributes the failure of the stove to draw properly to the remaining small tree "blocking the draft. If you want your stove to work properly, it'll have to come down. That's all I've got to say" (12).

Had the story ended there, the closing focus would have been on the absurd priest with his idiotic *idée fixe*. But in Powers' most successful stories, the drama always shapes the experience of the central intelligence; hence, the closure must focus on the Mother Superior. It does so on a note that resolves the action, but heightens the ironic ambiguity: "She felt the blood assembling in patches on her cheeks. 'Thank you, Father,' she said, and went quickly out of the kitchen, only wanting to get upstairs and wash the money off her hands" (12).

Insofar as the artist's task is to give perceivable form to a complex human experience, Powers has performed it consummately well. However, he has rarely concluded a story with such unresolvable ambiguities—"The Poor Thing" being another of those rare instances. Now the ending of "The Lord's Day" does not—and need not—make it clear whether the Mother Superior has failed in her responsibilities to the sisters and has once again, as seems her habit, fled to the sanctuary of her room; or, whether she has triumphed over her baser impulse to express her wrath and indignation, contrary to the spirit of her holy vows. The ambiguity is like that of the Church Militant, with its foundations in the earth and its spires pointing to heaven. The same structure must necessarily touch both earth and sky.

VI *"The Forks"*

This same paradox is at the heart of "The Forks," another study of parish life in which true piety is defeated by mundane but superior forces within the Church.[24] This time the conflict is between a socially liberal young curate who reads the *Catholic Worker* and a snobbish monsignor who associates with the manager of the First National Bank and who despises the curate's "conception of the priesthood [as] evangelical in the worst sense, barbaric, gross, and foreign to the mind of the Church" (132). However, even though Powers' characters clearly represent diametrically opposed views of what befits the Church, they are not mere abstract symbols, in spite of the fact that there is not a single word describing their physical appearance—height, weight, color of eyes, etc. Concreteness and individuality are achieved by telling nuances in the dialogue, as in the contrast between the Monsignor's pompous quoting of Latin clichés—"*Damnant quod non intelligunt*" (120)—and the priest's charged use of slang—"I guess hush money . . . is lousy" (135). There are also dramatic gestural details—"Monsignor . . . gave the rear left fender an amorous chuck and eased into the front seat" (124); and Father Eudex, spading up crosses, "removed his coat first, then his collar, and finally was down to his undershirt" (128).

Powers presents everything from the perspective of Father Eudex. No judgments are pronounced—"Father Eudex could hear the others . . . giving an account of their stewardship, but could not judge them" (141). Nevertheless, judgments from the point of view of the young priest are implicit in every dialogue and event. Even the idiom of the narrator, as in most of Powers' stories, is that of his central character: "Monsignor's car . . . was long and black and new like a politician's" (119). In fact, as in every clerical story examined thus far, the entire story could easily be converted into a first-person narrative by substituting the first-person pronoun every time Father Eudex is cited. It is thus clear that the narrator identifies with the young priest.

The author's attitude toward the two characters is expressed in the choice of their names. In selecting *Eudex*, Powers had in mind the Latin word *judex* ("judge"), meaning a person qualified to decide on the relative merits of anything.[25]

The sequence of events in the story is symmetrically arranged in a balanced structure, with Father Eudex's long meditation at the center:

EUDEX-MSGR DIALOGUE	EUDEX-WORKER	EUDEX-MSGR DIALOGUE	EUDEX-INVESTOR	EUDEX-MSGR DIALOGUE
(Eudex's subtle revolt)		(Eudex's overt revolt) & MEDITATION		(Eudex's symbolic revolt and defeat)

The opening dozen lines of the story embody the basic conflict and characterizations in swift, sure strokes. We know at once that Father Eudex is a hard-working priest who suffers insult and abuse with patience; he has been to say Mass at an orphanage, prepares to say his priestly office, and responds to the Monsignor's snide query about the treatment of his car with a calm, "No trouble, Monsignor" (119). The Monsignor, on the other hand, is a worldly snob: "For a moment Monsignor stood framed in the screen door, fumbling his watch fob as for a full-length portrait" (119). His first remark, moreover, is neither a polite greeting nor an enquiry about the orphanage, but an expression of concern for his sumptuous new automobile which he significantly refers to as "she."

In the dialogue concerning the Model A Ford which the young priest wants to buy in order to make his sick calls and trips to the orphanage without suffering the noblesse oblige of the Monsignor or "bumming rides from parishioners" (119), it soon becomes evident that their conflict is between *functional* and *symbolic* values. The Monsignor is primarily concerned with appearances, with "conspicuous consumption," and with the good opinion of such parishioners as Mr. Memmers of the First National Bank. Father Eudex assumes that it is not merely pride which motivates the Monsignor, but ambition—a futile one—to become Bishop. Eudex baits the Monsignor by horrifying him with the rumor that the current "crazy" and "socialistic" bishop (obviously a reference to the late Bishop Shiel of Chicago) is to be the next Archbishop. This subtle taunting of the Monsignor constitutes Father Eudex's rebellion and ends the first phase of the story.

A sharp contrast follows in the behavior of these two men of the cloth. The Monsignor drives ostentatiously through traffic halted by an Irish cop, a parishioner whom the Monsignor grandly ignores and to whom "it was evidently inconceivable . . . that the Monsignor should ever venture abroad unless to bear the Holy Viaticum, always racing with death" (125). Meanwhile, the young priest helps the overworked janitor dig up a huge formal garden ordered by the Monsignor. Father Eudex's shoveling dirt with Joe Whalen expresses his identity with the working classes—*he* can address the janitor as "Joe" in honest camaraderie, but from the mouth of the Monsignor it is presumptuous: "Whalen turned in on himself. '*Joe*—is it!' " (129). The young priest resents the Monsignor's command that he not labor in the garden—"It's not prudent" (128); but he submits to authority just as he had to his Aunt Hazel when he was a child —"I can't come out and play this afternoon, Joe, on account of my Monsignor won't let me" (130).

The middle dialogue between the two priests leads the conflict to a crisis and to Father Eudex's open revolt. "The Monsignor had broken wild curates before . . . and he would ride again" (136). He might get rid of the young priest by sending him off to a university, but "with your tendencies . . . and with the universities honeycombed with Communists . . . that would never do" (131). In a long meditation Father Eudex recalls the insults and abuses he has suffered from the Monsignor, who thoroughly disapproves of his manners and his social values: "he found Father Eudex reading the *Catholic Worker* one day and had not trusted him since" (132).

The crux of their conflict is symbolically focused in "the forks" of the title. Father Eudex, who simply does not know and does not care to know proper table etiquette, consistently ignores all the silverware except the single knife, spoon, and fork. The discussion of one social problem leads to another, and finally to the disposition of the checks being distributed to members of the Church by the Rival Tractor Company, a corporation which attempts to lure the church into an unholy alliance against the workers. Father Eudex interprets the checks as bribery for the Church's support in political and economic matters and as a technique for tax evasion. The curate "placed his knife next to his fork on the plate, adjusted them this way and that until they seemed to work a combination in his mind, to spring a lock which in turn enabled him to speak out" (135). He then announces that he would refuse to accept the check or that he might endorse it over to the labor union's strike relief fund—an act of outright revolt against the Monsignor's values. But the Monsignor, after hopelessly remonstrating with him, takes his leave of Father Eudex "with a laugh"—confident of his ultimate triumph.

While the Monsignor is taking a nap, a widow of the parish comes to consult the Church on an important matter. Father Eudex interrupts the reading of his Office to talk to her. First she unwittingly reveals her anti-Semitic prejudices by carefully explaining that her name, Klein, is not a "Jew name," and then asks for advice on how best to invest the money she has inherited from her husband: "Klein always said, 'If you got a problem, Freda, see the priest'" (137). When Father Eudex gives her the classic Christian advice to give it to the poor, she becomes highly indignant and demands to see his "boss." Eudex advises her to return in the evening when the Monsignor can no doubt give her the information she wants.

As Eudex goes to his room, the Monsignor enquires, "Who was it?"; and Eudex ironically replies, "A woman seeking good counsel" (140). In his room he tears up the Rival Tractor Company check and flushes it down the toilet; but this act of revolt, like that of the Mother Superior in "The Lord's Day," is heavily charged with a sense of frustration and defeat. "He went to his room and stood looking out the window at nothing" (141); he has nothing to show for his efforts—in his own terms or the Church's. Though he cannot judge the other priests for their various compromises and justifications in spending the money for good causes, his own act is implicit condemnation of them. Any use of "hush money" is cooperation with the iniquity of mammon. There is an ironic contrast between his thinking that he could not judge his brother priests and the Monsignor's earlier warning that he must watch his behavior: "*Damnant quod non intelligunt*" (120).

It is not true, as Robert Heilman claims, that " 'The Forks' does not have a plot in the conventional sense of the word,"[26] for there is a clear movement from conflict to climax, defeat, and denouement—all quite traditional. Rarely cited by reviewers of *Prince of Darkness,* the story does lack the rich humor usually found in Powers' stories, and its irony rasps a bit. But "The Forks" extends our understanding of "the endless struggle between religious idealism and selfish, worldly interests" which is central to Powers' vision.

VII The Presence of Grace

With the exception of "Lions, Harts . . ." the five clerical stories in *Prince of Darkness* are variations on the theme of priestly venality. Powers' second collection, *The Presence of Grace,* is—as its title would suggest—a shift in emphasis from the negative to the positive. None of the seven clerical stories in the second collection has as a central character a "prince of darkness." In fact, as we have already seen, two of the later stories dealing with the satanic Father Burner show him well on the way to redeeming himself. Between the two books, Powers mellowed; his wit lost something of its aggressive edge; and, though he still had a sharp eye for the foibles and weaknesses of the clergy and the inevitable ironies and paradoxes that are attendant upon men of flesh who elect to live lives of the spirit, there is always in these new stories at least some fragment of grace shored against the ruin.[27]

As time went by, Powers moved more and more away from the issues raised by the depression, the war, and the racial revolution to devote himself more to the rectory and its environs. In that humble arena he discovered the greatest spiritual conflicts and problems. Of the nine stories which Powers published in the 1950's, only two ("Blue Island" and "Look How the Fish Live") have a secular setting and orientation—and neither of those stories has the racial or political subject of his earlier secular stories. No story more clearly signals the metamorphosis than "The Presence of Grace." It is as if Powers were looking with detached amusement at his younger, cockier self, the young radical with such militant convictions, with such certainty that he knew where the significant issues lay, and with such intolerance of the obvious forces of evil and injustice that he in fact lacked charity in judging the human frailties of his more conservative characters.

The title story of *The Presence of Grace* is, as is typical of Powers, divided in three sections and presents a crucial day in the life of the central character, as seen from his point of view. Father Fabre at breakfast cannot elicit more than a grumpy "no" from his pastor when he enquires whether it isn't too late, or otherwise inadvisable, to administer a Legion of Decency pledge to the parishioners. Simply deny everything is the pastor's way of dealing with all difficult questions. That afternoon, against the vague warnings of the rectory housekeeper but with the encouragement of the janitor, Father Fabre accepts an invitation to dinner at Mrs. Mathers', a widow who belongs to the Altar and Rosary Society. There he finds the other company to be a crusty widower and his inane daughter—both non-Catholics; and he is stunned to discover that the man is actually living in Mrs. Mathers' flat. He feels that he has been used to give his blessing to an adulterous relationship and flees back to the rectory, only to find that Grace Halloran, who had refused an invitation to the same dinner, is leading a group of the altar ladies in a protest to the pastor. Will he tolerate the fact that his curate lends the dignity of the Church to the relationship between Mrs. Mathers and Mr. Pint? Now Father Fabre feels humble in the presence of the pastor's apparent grace when the pastor simply dissipates the charges against Mrs. Mathers with his grumpy "*'S not so!*" (187).

More than a dozen critics concur in seeing the pastor as the hero of the story. Granville Hicks says, "The old pastor unexpectedly wins our admiration,"[28] and Naomi Lebowitz adds that Grace Halloran's "petty and perverted interpretation . . . is overcome by the spiritual presence of grace in the stubborn pastor, who is visually elevated from dormouse to shepherd."[29] Other critics all agree.[30]

Only the shrewdly skeptical Evelyn Waugh demurs: " 'Presence of Grace' goes deeper into the sacerdotal function, bringing the cure of souls into proper perspective among the more mundane activities of the parish priest. It left me in some doubt about the precise significance of the pastor's simple negation."[31] It should, for Father Fabre's mind is not simply the medium through which we see the pastor's "triumph over the scandals of the Nervous Nellies"; his mind is rather the arena of the most significant action—the discovery of his own Philistinism and his humble imputation of grace to a chuckleheaded priest. Father Fabre is wrong in seeing the pastor as a faithful shepherd, but his error is in itself a sign of the grace within him.

Though Father Fabre is not characterized with so much depth of background or in so many varied situations as Father Eudex in "The Forks," he remains a simpler version of the dogmatic young liberal in confrontation with unyielding authority in the Church. But the technique of "The Presence of Grace" is as relaxed as a flowing brook compared with "The Lord's Day," which was a taut spring unwinding inside a complex mechanism. The relaxed and casual tone of "The Presence of Grace" is signalled by the opening lines: "On a fine Sunday morning in June, Father Fabre opened the announcement book to familiarize himself with the names of the deceased in the parish for whom Masses would be offered in the coming week" (163).

Throughout the story the rhythms of the prose indicate the moods of the curate. When tensions do occur, the prose tightens: "It wasn't a well-run parish. The pastor was a hard man to interest in a problem. They saw each other at meals" (163). In the opening scene, the conflict between the curate and the pastor over the Legion of Decency pledge has faint overtones of the socio-political problem in "The Forks," but it proves to be no more than a gambit for presenting contrasting personalities rather than for raising an important narrative issue.

Father Fabre has no difficulty in making the right moral judgment about the Legion of Decency pledge; but he is shown to be rather callow in the subtler, more complex issues of individual personal relations. He cannot cope with the petty feuding of the janitor and the housekeeper: "'I don't blame you for being sore at her, Father.' ('I'm not,' Father Fabre murmured, but John, drinking, smiled into his cup.) 'I told her it's your business what you do. "He's old enough," I said . . . Hell, you know how these old maids are, Father . . . Just needs a man. *You* can understand that'" (168). And if poor Miss Burke needs a man, what must be the urgency of the widow, Mrs. Mathers, who is so pathetically desperate for the sexagenarian Mr. Pint that she schemes for his conversion and risks her reputation among the ladies of the Altar Society. But Father Fabre fails to give her enough credit for piety—the absence of Grace from the dinner table is as much his loss as anyone else's. Grace would not even communicate with him on the telephone! His embarrassment and confusion are marvelously rendered in a hilarious episode involving Mr. Pint.

> "That's a good idea of yours when you make ice cream—bringing an extra shirt, I mean."
>
> There was a bad silence, the worst of the afternoon, crippling every tongue. . . . Mr. Pint was positively stony. Finally, as if seeing no other way, Mrs. Mathers explained:
>
> "Mr. Pint lives here, Father."
>
> "He does?"
>
> "Yes, Father."
>
> "I guess I didn't know."
>
> "I guess I didn't tell you."
>
> "No reason why you should've," he said quickly. "You do have quite a bit of room here." He seemed to be perspiring. "Certainly do get the sun." (177).

He is nonplussed even by the moronic Velma, Mr. Pint's daughter, who is no Catholic, "but I see all your movies . . . I liked *The Miracle of the Bells* the best" (174). She cannot understand why Father Fabre doesn't date girls and is quite sure that the married priests she once met weren't *Old* Catholics at all!

On his return to the rectory, Father Fabre finds the incensed old ladies of the Altar and Rosary Society—the very ones whom the crusty pastor had praised: "Nuns could not have kept the church cleaner, and the good ladies, unlike nuns, didn't labor under the illusion that they were somehow priests, only different, and so weren't always trying to vault the communion rail to the altar" (183). In penance for failing to heed the housekeeper's warning about Mrs. Mathers' invitation, Father Fabre drinks "Miss Burke's foul coffee to the dregs and chewed up a few grounds" (185) and gives his account of the afternoon to the old man who listened with eyes "blue, blank and blue" (185). And when the old pastor maintains his silence before the irate ladies, Father Fabre falls victim to a smug conviction of his own superiority—*he* would not have been afraid; *he* would have dispersed them with contempt: "with chapter and verse he'd atomize 'em. *This day thou shouldst be pastor*" (186). But when the pastor confounds the ladies with his taciturnity and his repeated grunt, " 'S not so," Father Fabre realizes the absurdity and self-degradation of his own suspicion of Mrs. Mathers and comes to feel that "the way for pastors was ever lit by the flares of special grace . . . his heart humbled himself with thoughts of his unworthiness" (190).

But the astute reader will bear in mind that this is Father Fabre's judgment—not the author's. There is no objective evidence of the pastor's superior insight or special grace. In fact, he is rather obviously employing his habitual tactic of simply refusing to acknowledge anything, true or false, that might cause any difficulty or embarrassment. As in the beginning of the story, when he insisted that he had not ruined Father Fabre's chasuble with a flick of ink—" 'S not ink!"—he was avoiding responsibility on the specious technicality that his pen was filled with *Quink*. "He escaped much of the man's fate. Instead of arguing his way out of a jam, or confessing himself in error, the pastor simply denied everything" (165). It isn't the pastor who has changed or revealed a hidden grace; it is Father Fabre who, because he can impute such a quality to the pastor, emerges as the better man and better priest. This action foreshadows that of many of the subsequent clerical stories and of *Morte D'Urban*.

VIII *Other Priests and Bishops*

A similar spiritual movement is involved in an amusing companion story, "A Losing Game," in which once again Father Fabre proves his own grace in conceding victory to the old pastor. The closest thing to slapstick comedy or pure farce in all of Powers' writing, the story nevertheless has a serious point. Unable to extricate the pastor from his magpie's nest of a room to select a suitable typewriter table from the locked warehouse in the cellar, Father Fabre tricks the janitor into summoning him by threatening to force the lock. Then, armed with air rifles against the rats, the two conduct a mad safari through piles of junk. Father Fabre cannily feigns indifference to a beautiful maple table and pretends to be unworthy of a horrid mohair chair which the pastor offers him.

Suddenly Fabre is struck in the leg by a pellet which the pastor fires at a rat. After driving himself to the hospital in the rectory car (which the pastor magnanimously gives him permission to use), Father Fabre suggests in vain that the wound might have to be reported to the police. Upon his return to the rectory, he is puzzled by the coy silence of the pastor and the janitor until he enters his room and finds the dusty old mohair chair awaiting him: "They clearly hadn't done a thing to the chair. The dust was all there, every grain intact. They were waiting for him, the pastor and John, waiting to see him sitting in it" (106).

The story might have concluded with Father Fabre's utter defeat in trying to outwit the cagy old curmudgeon and his subtle Slav janitor. But Powers' new mood in the rectory stories compels him to add one more revolution to the movement of the story—toward Father Fabre's spiritual victory over his own vindictive anger and resentment. And he does it without violating the sustained comic tone of the whole: "He thought of disappointing them, of holing up as the pastor had earlier. But he just couldn't contend with the man any more that day. He didn't know how he'd ever be able to thank them, John for carrying it up from the basement, the pastor for the thing itself, but he limped over to the door to let them in. Oh, it was a losing game" (106). One must not, of course, convert this very funny story into a serious parable; but it is relevant to observe the paradox: it is, and it isn't, a losing game.

Powers' genial disposition does not forsake him when he moves into the upper echelons of the Church hierarchy—from the humble parish priests of the rectory to His Eminence, the Bishop of the Diocese. In "Zeal" he adds another memorable portrait to his gallery of obtuse, well-meaning, bungling priests who nevertheless somehow manage to provoke their smug superiors into a redeeming examination of their own souls. The superior in "Zeal" is a bored, sophisticated bishop whose hope for a quiet journey is shattered when he finds himself entrained with an officious busybody priest who is leading a group of tourist pilgrims to Rome. The opening dialogue quickly establishes the character and attitude of the Bishop and Father Early (who cheerfully reveals that in the seminary they called him "Crazy Early"). The Bishop tries to remain aloof as Father Early attacks the clerical privilege of traveling in parlor cars at coach rates:

> Father Early had a nose like a parrot's and something on it like psoriasis that held the Bishop's attention—unfortunately, for Father Early seemed to think it was his talk. . . .
>
> ". . . I fear privilege more than persecution. Of course the one follows the other, as the night the day."
>
> "Is it true, Father, that there are rattlesnakes along here?" . . . "There must be a cave for you up there, somewhere, Father." (130-31)

But after accepting a piece of fudge which Father Early offers to all the pilgrims ("Divinity? Divinity?" [133]), the Bishop feels obliged to stay with Father Early at least as far as Chicago —not knowing that he will be committed to an even greater ordeal.

Because the point of view is that of the Bishop, we get a prominently highlighted view of the pesky priest, but only suppressed glimpses and innuendos concerning the pompous Bishop himself. Hearing that Monsignor Reed had evaded his responsibilities to the pilgrims, the Bishop considers, "Would Reed do this to him? Reed had done this to him. Reed had once called the Bishop's diocese the next thing to a titular see" (134). At lunch the zealot ploys him into acting as guide to an elderly American Gothic couple during the stopover in Chicago, and the Bishop is so preoccupied with his own bad luck that it never occurs to him that the penniless couple are petrified at the possible expenses of sight-seeing: "Mr. Doyle, watching the meter, said, 'These things could sure cost you' " (138).

The Bishop is not reprieved by the change of trains, for apparently travel agents book all men of the cloth together. He finds himself involved in an inane dialogue between Father Early and a young couple at dinner—tipping is an evil; Watts' name on light bulbs and Galvan's on garbage cans attest to Catholic interest in progress; Chesterton's choice for desert-island reading was a manual on shipbuilding. The crisis of the story occurs when the young couple leave and Father Early expresses his suspicions and anxiety about the young man who, he is sure, has been drinking, is in the clutches of a harlot, and is a Catholic: "In the Bishop's opinion, it was none of Father Early's business. He knew what Father Early was getting at, and he didn't like it. Father Early was thinking of taking on more trouble" (143).

But the Bishop becomes concerned in spite of himself; late that evening, unable to sleep, he goes to the club car where he finds Father Early engaged in a weary siege of small talk to keep the young man from the harlot's compartment: "What an intricate instrument for good a simple man could be! Perhaps Father Early was only a fool, a ward of Heaven, not subject to the usual penalties for meddling. No, it was zeal, and people, however far gone, still expected it from a man of God. But, even so, Father Early ought to be more careful, humbler before the mystery of iniquity. And still . . ." (145). This "and still" shows that the Bishop has taken the bait; but, not yet hooked, he allows the young man to flee when Father Early is forced to leave him to go to the toilet. Entering his Pullman car, the Bishop observes the young man entering the girl's room, and that hooks him. He is able to sleep only after conceding to himself that Father Early "on his feet and trying . . . was what counted in the sight of God, not success. *Thinkest thou that I cannot ask my Father, and he will give me presently more than twelve legions of angels?*" (146).

The next day, the Bishop assumes responsibility for Monsignor Reed's group of pilgrims. As John P. Sisk astutely observes, "here we must face the . . . disturbing irony of the value for good and good intentions that may produce harmful results in a man who is still a bore and ought to be 'humbler before the mystery of iniquity.' And we must hold in mind also the fact that the Bishop has seen in Father Early's extravagance of zeal his own deficiency."[32] Father Early, in his zealous search for evils to combat, is something of the reverse of the pastor in "The Presence of Grace," who sought only to avoid trouble by the simple denial of its existence. It would be naïve to see positive virtue in either. Simple-mindedness and lack of insight—as, for example, in Brother Titus of "Lions, Harts . . ."—can never be marks of the best priest. Father Early's deficiencies in this respect are clear; this great crusader against tipping feels no qualms about accepting a regular supply of cigars from a grateful parishioner whom he had cured of alcoholism. But even a grotesque simulacrum of piety can arouse the genuine thing in the spirit of a man who is capable of searching his own soul.

This same psycho-moral action occurs in "Dawn," the last of Powers' clerical stories of the 1950's. In this story Powers introduces the fictional Diocese of Great Plains, later the setting for *Morte D'Urban*; its central characters also reappear in the novel—Father Bruno Udovic, the Chancellor of the Diocese, who in the novel is pastor of St. Monica's; Monsignor James Renton, Dean of the Cathedral, Father Urban's best friend and confidant; and the Bishop himself, here unnamed, but in the novel the Bishop Conor whose golf club becomes a lethal weapon. But "Dawn" is not one of Powers' most successful efforts because it lacks the unity of time, the taut structure, the ironic imagery, and the foreshadowing that in other stories make the protagonist's final conversion credible.

Father Udovic is a dolt who, as some of the men in the parishes maintained, landed his job "only because he employed the touch system of typing" (15). Against Monsignor Renton's objections, he has pushed ahead the Peter's Pence collection so that the Bishop can personally deliver it to the Pope during his impending visit to Rome. But Father Udovic is distressed to find in the collection plate a sealed envelope addressed to His Holiness and marked "Personal." He fears what it might contain—at the worst "all manner of filth, spelled out in letters snipped from newsprint and calculated to shake Rome's faith in him" (19). Though the Bishop is "very anxious that not too much be made of the matter," he shifts the envelope about his desk for weeks while Father Udovic tries to locate the sender through announcements from the pulpits and a memorandum in the diocesan paper.

Just before the Bishop is to leave for Rome, Monsignor Renton sends the culprit, a sullen and taciturn widow, to the diocesan office; and Father Udovic is soon convinced that the Monsignor has done so merely to "get even" with him for having forced through an early Peter's Pence collection. Under cross-examination, Mrs. Anton explains her motives for placing her one-dollar contribution in a sealed envelope personally addressed to the Pope:

> ". . . I don't want somebody else takin' all the credit with the Holy Father. . . !"
>
> "Why don't you send it by regular mail?"
>
> "He'd never see it! That's why! Some flunky'd get hold of it! Same as here! Oh, don't I know!"
>
> The Bishop walked out, leaving them together—with the envelope. (22)

Had the story concluded on that note, it would have been typical of the earlier clerical stories in *Prince of Darkness* in which the unworthy priest is trapped and humiliated by his own moral failing. But true to his mellower mood, Powers tacks on a not very credible final paragraph in which Father Udovic is made to experience insight and humility:

> In the next few moments, although Father Udovic knew he had an obligation to instruct Mrs. Anton, and had the text for it—"When thou dost an alms-deed, sound not a trumpet before thee"—he despaired. He realized that they had needed each other to arrive at their sorry state. It seemed to him, sitting there saying nothing, that they saw each other as two people who'd sinned together on earth might see each other in hell, unchastened even then, only blaming each other for what had happened. (22-23)

Mrs. Anton's role in "Dawn" proves to be the same as that of Father Fabre's crusty pastor in "The Presence of Grace" and of Father Early in "Zeal"—a person whose serious deficiencies in the pursuit of piety provoke a saving insight in the central character of the story.

IX *"The Devil Was the Joker"*

There remains one more story from *The Presence of Grace*, "The Devil Was the Joker," which explicitly foreshadows the novel, *Morte D'Urban*, because of the creation of the fictional Order of St. Clement. Though neither of its two central characters—Myles Flynn, an innocent ex-seminarian, and Mr. McMaster, a tricky traveling salesman for the Clementines—is a priest, the pattern of moral action resembles that of the clerical stories.

Separated from his wife, Mr. McMaster, a convalescent alcoholic and a hernia case, is "fat and fifty or so, with a candy-pink face, sparse orange hair, and popeyes" (61). When he invites the night orderly, Myles Flynn—"a cradle Catholic"—to work with him as a traveling promoter of the *Clementine*, a publication of the Order of St. Clement, each conceals from the other his true motive for agreeing to the liaison. However, because Myles is the point-of-view character, we know his reasons almost at once, and we learn Mac's reasons only gradually as Myles comes to understand them. Though he doesn't think much of the Clementine Fathers, Myles needs only a moment's consideration before accepting Mac's proposition; he sees the work as a means of meeting a pastor or a bishop who might arrange for him to enroll again in a seminary. Doing so is urgent because he may at any time be drafted for service in the Korean War. On his side, Mac, who hides the fact that he is not even a Catholic but a "bloody Orangeman," needs a low-paid chauffeur and assistant in selling religious—and non-religious—articles to the clergy.

But a very crucial factor in their relationship, introduced in the beginning of the story, is never explicitly clarified:

> Myles said he'd been four years in a seminary, studying for the priesthood—until "something happened."
>
> There he stopped.
>
> Mr. McMaster grinned. "To make a long story short," he said.
>
> Myles shook his head. He'd told Mr. McMaster all there was for him to tell—all he knew. He'd simply been asked to leave, he said. (61-62)

Mac apparently understands at once that Myles may be referring to some homosexual episode—and is attracted to him all the more for that very reason. Later, on their travels, "Myles and Mac were staying together in the same hotels, and Myles . . . felt slightly kept. Mac only wanted him handy late at night, it seemed, so as to have someone with whom to take his pleasure, which was haranguing" (81)—or so Myles thinks. But he is puzzled and wonders if he has brought on this bizarre relationship through some fault of his own: "He was someone whom people looking for trouble always seemed to find. It had happened to him in the hospital, in the seminary, in the Boy Scouts. If a million people met in one place, and he was there, he was certain the worst of them would rise as a man and make for him" (81). On one occasion Mac buys Myles a Hawaiian sports shirt, and on another orders a night clerk to let him into Myles' room because he thinks Myles might be sick—" 'I love that boy,' he proclaimed" (81). The language and details of such passages suggest that Myles is unaware of Mac's homosexual passion for him.

As they travel together in Mac's 1941 Cadillac, the salesman's small talk about medical cures, funerals, and other mundane topics only provokes the ex-seminarian's views on the corporal works of mercy and the blessed work of the medieval burial confraternities. Though their concerns differed, "they were like two men in a mine, working at different levels, in different veins, and lost to each other" (67). Gradually, however, Myles comes to learn more and more of Mac's shady devices and shoddy goods. He finds especially reprehensible Mac's tactic of eliciting the favor of a stubborn pastor by "taking the pledge" from him and then getting him to promote the *Clementine* during services. But Myles remains with Mac, for Mac seems genuinely friendly toward him; and, besides, there is always hope of meeting a bishop.

At one rectory, while Mac is upstairs playing blackjack with the priests (of whom Mac later says, "a den of thieves. I'm pretty sure I was taken" [87]), Myles is harangued by a zealous curate to seek out a bishop on his own: "the Clementines were a corny outfit, and no bishop in his right mind, seeing Myles with Mac, would ever take a chance on him" (85). The climax of the story occurs the next day when Myles announces that he is quitting and explains his motives for having undertaken the work in the first place. He cannot understand Mac's powerful desperation to keep him: "Could Mac want so badly for an underpaid chauffeur . . . what he wanted still more, it was becoming clear, was to have a boon companion" (89).

In a drunken outburst, Mac threatens to report Myles to the draft board, confesses that he isn't a Catholic, and seeks to exploit Myles' proselytizing zeal by accepting a Catholic Bible from him in preference to the King James version supplied by the Gideons. On the next morning he tries his most desperate tactic—he urges Myles to baptize him. But Myles magnificently resists the temptation to play priest. He sees that Mac is "the serpent, the nice old serpent with Glen-plaid markings, who wasn't *very* poisonous," and catches him "with the forked stick just behind the head" (94). Though Mac cajoles, whines, and pleads, Myles is adamant; and finally Mac is gone: "He'd left a small deposit of gray ash on the rug near the spot where he'd coiled and uncoiled" (95). Thus, in denying to himself the role of priest, Myles proves more than ever worthy of it by having exorcised the devil.

In "The Devil Was the Joker" the dramatic action reaches its climax when the fervently pious ex-seminarian is tempted to perform the sacrament of baptism. To be sure, the act has power and meaning in strictly psychological ("man-to-man") terms. But any sacrament also invokes a theological ("man-to-God") dimension; and once again Powers is, in the highest literary sense, ambiguous. In fact, his special genius is that, for perceptive readers, he always invests seemingly ordinary and realistic events with profound spiritual meanings. In this respect, his literary structures are like the double-patterns created by the Gestalt psychologists (the Rubin vase) which, depending on what portions of the image are taken as figure or ground, can be seen as a Greek urn or as two profiles looking at each other, without any change occurring in the structure itself.

The few reviewers of *The Presence of Grace* who did not ignore "The Devil Was the Joker" generally saw it as a tale "of low-life through the presbytery key-hole"[33] and relished the realistic satire in such passages as the following:

> The package deal always began with Mac's opening his bag of tricks. It was a Gladstone bag, which he had got from a retired cookie salesman. When open, it looked like a little stadium, and where the cookies had once been on display . . . there were now rosaries, medals, scapulars—religious goods of the usual quality, which didn't catch the eye in many rectories. . . . Mac had a new kind of rosary, too. It was made of plastic, to fit the hand, and in function and appearance it was similar to an umpire's ball-and-strike indicator. Each time a little key was punched, the single dial, which showed the Mysteries—Sorrowful, Joyful, and Glorious—revolved a notch, and for the Ave Marias there was a modest tick, for the Pater Nosters an authoritative click . . . *not* to replace the old model, . . . but to facilitate prayer while driving, for the new rosary was easily attached to the steering wheel. "Of course, you still have to say the prayers," Mac would say. (72-73)

The sure hand of a master satirist is at work here; but once we realize that what is being satirized is the mechanization and commercialization of prayer—and not prayer itself—we are back in the realm of the spiritual. Powers' satire always has an implied positive standard of values, and he mocks deviations from that standard. However difficult it may be to define with precision, the constant standard in Powers' fiction is the true Christian spirit, so that even when two or more central characters are "variables" no real confusion should result. Since all of his stories are presented through the consciousness of one of the characters, and since the true Christian spirit involves a humility (not to be confused with simple-mindedness) which would prevent that character's awareness of his own sanctity, his state of grace cannot be explicitly revealed. For him to rejoice in it would automatically be evidence of pride, which negates holiness. Often the character feels so smug about his superiority to another that he is unconscious of his own deficiencies until some dramatic event shocks him into awareness and humility.

His *felix culpa,* however, is not balanced by a rise in stature of his foil, as many critics seem to think. Alfred Kazin, for example, says: "Often the drama does not develop quite as one had expected: in 'The Presence of Grace,' the old pastor unexpectedly wins our admiration, as in 'The Devil Was the Joker' the salesman of religious specialties wins our sympathy. But the reversal is never mechanical, *it always grows out of a deeper perception of character.*"[34] Kazin is wrong, for these foil characters are *not* more deeply perceived in the end, nor are they at all changed. What changes is the attitude of the point-of-view protagonist who comes to think more kindly of the other. Father Fabre fails in the end to see that the taciturn old codger who is his pastor is still ducking the issues; but he is so humbled by the discovery of his own moral failing that the former object of his derision now seems shrewder and wiser. Similarly, Myles Flynn fails to realize that McMaster probably has a homosexual attraction to him, but he is so moved by the pathos of Mac's desperation that he cannot be vindictive. However, the grace that blinds the protagonist to the faults of others need not blind the reader or critic.[35]

X *"Keystone"*

In May, 1963, two months after he received the National Book Award for *Morte D'Urban*, Powers published in the *New Yorker* an eleven thousand word novella, "Keystone." Depicting the rise of Father Gau, a power-driven priest (like Urban before his fall), this work is a fascinating companion piece to the novel; equally subtle in structure, characterizations, and symbolism, the story is perhaps a bit too compressed to achieve the same large dramatic force. In "Keystone," a variation on the theme of power-politics within a chancery, the action is seen from the point of view of the go-getter's victim—the bumbling, ineffectual old Bishop John Dullinger of Ostergothenburg, whose portrait was among those that adorned the wall at St. Clement's Hill and whose strange diocese, just west of Great Plains, Father Urban once visited for twenty-four hours.[36]

The story is neatly structured. A brief opening scene depicts the frustrations of Bishop Dullinger with his aged Vicar-General, Monsignor Holstein—an old friend and fussy Jansenist who, though successful "with public events of a devotional nature," was completely ineffectual in influencing the secular life of the community. Upon the death of Father Scuza of New Pilsen, Monsignor Holstein expects that, as usual, he will be able to determine who will be the new pastor, but he finds that he himself is farmed out to the distant parish. To take his place as Chancellor of the Cathedral and personal chauffeur, Bishop Dullinger appoints a young rural pastor, Father Gau, who responds to the summons with, "Gee, Your Excellency!"

There follows a two-part exposition, first relating how earlier in the year the Bishop was greeted by a children's choir on his confirmation trip to Grasshopper Lake (Father Gau's parish) and how on a later visit to the parish harvest festival he was impressed by Father Gau's vigilance over the beer stand. Thus, Father Gau was invited to the Chancery where he promptly began to make himself indispensable. At nightly sessions over Benedictine and cigars at Webb's Hotel, the Bishop waxed reminiscent over his long cigar to the obbligato of Father Gau's "Gee's!"

Gradually Father Gau manipulates the Bishop into relaxing Monsignor Holstein's strict fasting regulations, prompts him to attend banquets, engage in civic affairs, write a column for the diocesan paper, and in general become so active that he must delegate other diocesan business to Father Gau, who—no longer chauffeur—is made a Monsignor and Rector of the Cathedral and domestic prelate with three curates of his own.

Then the central action of the drama begins with a discussion of Monsignor Holstein's suggestion that the large cemetery cross be relocated so that it will be more visible from the highway. Monsignor Gau makes the bold suggestion that the entire cemetery be moved to an abandoned airport (where apparently there will be no more rising on high) to allow for the building of a new cathedral and the development of an upper-class housing sub-division. The Bishop, having anticipated an easy old age, is understandably reluctant to engage in such a venture; but Monsignor Gau's wiles maneuver him into it. He is the actual executant—managing the legal affairs and hiring architects and contractors while the Bishop stands around looking important and gradually becoming more and more bewildered by the complexity of the operations and the modernity of the cathedral design. But he soon becomes aroused and reacts peevishly to the smooth stone facade (he wanted rough fieldstones), the low structure (he wanted a medieval height), and the lack of keystones in the arches. He asserts his authority in petty and futile gestures—stopping the sale of sweatshirts bearing his coat of arms and abandoning his column in the diocesan paper.

The climax comes with the dedication of the new cathedral attended by bishops, archbishops, and even an indigent Italian cardinal—all invited by Monsignor Gau. In the humid heat, Bishop Dullinger becomes exhausted during the course of his long, dull sermon, and Monsignor Gau leads the guests on the grand tour and presides over the ceremonial banquet. The denouement comes a month later when the Bishop, while mulling over ways and means of getting rid of his arrogant Rector and reasserting his own authority, receives word that Monsignor Gau has been appointed Auxiliary Bishop.

The style of "Keystone" is vintage Powers: the limited point of view, the colloquial idiom of the narrative voice, and the technique of the ironic double-take: "The bishop peeked into the bag, said 'Oh,' and, with a nod, thanked Monsignor Holstein for his kindness—for the fine new appointment book. *It was that time of year again.*" And the characterizations are rendered, not by lists of adjectives, but by means of sharp and vividly evocative dramatizations of their behavior:

> On mornings when there was clear and present danger in the diocese—a dance for ninth graders scheduled for the Eagles' Hall, "Martin Luther" coming to the Orpheum—Monsignor Holstein sat down and beat himself about his black shoes and white socks with the Minneapolis *Tribune,* while the Bishop, a stocky man, opened and shut his mouth like a fish. If the matter was one the Bishop really cared about, he said, "Brr-jorrk-brrr." On such mornings, by the time the Bishop got the paper it was in poor shape and so was he.

Confronted with such brilliant and incisive writing, it is difficult to imagine how a critic could say of "Keystone" that "its plot is not especially entertaining, nor its characters significantly different. . . . The new story is (neither) so closely knit, nor so subtle as previous offerings."[37] Such is the verdict of Father John J. Kirvan, the only critic who has thus far dealt with "Keystone." Nevertheless, he finds it to be a "serious" and "skillful" story, especially for the symbolism involved in the building of a new cathedral, which illuminates "not only this story but the entire body of Powers' work." Focusing on those symbols which might be translated into theological abstractions, Father Kirvan finds the meaning—of this and all of Powers' writing—to be that "the Church is being made over in the image and likeness of the corporation, its stability resting upon organization, its prestige on locality, and its value on optical illusion."

And, indeed, seen from that perspective, significant elements of the story bear him out.[38] The arch of the modern church does not have an apex of a single stone upon which all the other stones lean and from which they gain strength. Support is now dependent upon a framework of steel: "keystones in the arches would have clashed with the architect's over-all plan." Furthermore, the church which once soared vertically toward God, its traditional source of authority, is now a horizontal structure spreading outwards toward the community and the society. The Bishop "wasn't getting as high a structure as he'd wanted at first, but, as Monsignor Gau pointed out to him, the site would do a lot for the cathedral." And the contractor earnestly reassures the Bishop that "it'll be good for fifty, seventy-five—maybe a hundred—years." Nor is the cathedral to be constructed of "plain, ordinary everyday stones, just as they came from the hand of God." The final irony is that it will be set upon a deconsecrated cemetery!

The symbolism of the cathedral's structure becomes quite pointed during the feud between the architects and the contractors. The former insist that it resembles a chasuble; the latter, a coffin. "It looked like neither, the Bishop thought, and it never would unless you viewed it from above, from an airplane"—and there is the Powers' ironic double-take again. Of course, no one in the story ever does view it "from above," for the airport has been abandoned.[39]

Such details seem to support Father Kirvan's more or less allegorical reading of the story as "a profound and disturbing portrait of the Church in the United States." Yet, however attractive it must be for a man of the cloth to see "more" than merely "a character study of two men, the aging bishop and the young and ambitious Father Gau," there are two serious objections to his interpretation. The first has to do with the adequacy of his version of the allegory, and the second with the serious limitations of allegory itself as a mode of literary art.

As an allegory, "Keystone" can hardly be read simply as the usurpation of the true, spiritual Church by a secularly-oriented bureaucracy dedicated to managerial efficiency and suburban class values; for the "old Church"—in the persona of Bishop

John Dullinger—is hardly depicted as worthy of survival. In fact, it succumbs to the likes of Father Gau precisely because it has long since lost its spiritual force and vitality. Presided over by a fuddy-duddy Bishop inclined toward ease and a Jansenist Vicar-General aroused to a vigorous defense of the faith only by banning teen-age dances, Italian films, and the Kinsey Report, the church is already a moribund institution before Father Gau arrives on the scene. In this connection, it is symbolically appropriate that the Vicar-General's annual Christmas gift to his Bishop is an appointment book that contains, among other helpful hints, the "Good Rules for Businessmen" by which the "Bishop examined his conscience":

> Don't worry; don't overbuy; don't go security.
> Keep your vitality up; keep insured; keep sober; keep cool.
> Stick to chosen pursuits, but not to chosen methods.
> Be content with small beginnings and develop them.
> Be wary of dealing with unsuccessful men.
> Be cautious, but when a bargain is made stick to it.
> Keep down expenses, but don't be stingy.
> Make friends, but not favorites.
> Don't take new risks to retrieve old losses.
> Stop a bad account at once.
> Make plans ahead, but don't make them in cast iron.
> Don't tell what you are to do until you have done it.

The most relevant of these rules would seem to be "Keep your vitality up" and "Stick to chosen pursuits, but not to chosen methods"—injunctions the Bishop has hardly heeded. The problem for the Church—and for Father Kirvan—would seem to be that, faced with a realization that it has lost its vitality and its true pursuit, the Church must rid itself of its Monsignor Holsteins (who merely chew the cud of ritual but fail to provide the milk of salvation). But, in seeking renewal, it must not put its trust in go-getters like Father Gau. The "old" Church will no longer serve; the "new" Church will merely put on a socially acceptable façade of service.

Powers has not presented in this story a positive alternative—in the person of a figure like Pope John XXIII or an event like the Ecumenical Council. Hence, the story as a commentary on the state of the Church is even more disturbing than Father

Kirvan sees it; for we do not, as he believes, "see the Church surrendering its *rightful* dignity and influence for the counterfeit status of urban America." We see instead a Church that has long since lost any claim to dignity succumbing easily to a bloodless *coup d'église.*

There may, however, be some hope, as suggested in the imagery of the indelible cross which occurs at the end of the story and which suggests that the Church is indestructible. Somehow it will survive the sordid victory of Monsignor Gau and the bitter defeat of the Bishop:

> . . . the Bishop stood for some time before a chart on the wall . . . [which] showed the spiritual plan of the diocese: bishop at the top of the tree, vicar-general below him, then chancellor, and then to the right, in the right branch, clergy in general, and to the left, on the left branch, sisters, or religious, as they were designated on the chart, and, finally, down the middle, on the trunk of the tree, the laity. The Bishop hadn't really looked at the cross for years, and now saw it as he never had before. . . . He hadn't noticed it before, . . . but the chancellor occupied the very heart of the cross. . . . It seemed to him that it gave a distorted view of the spiritual plan of the diocese. He tried one of the thumbtacks, then another. When he had the chart down, he carried it around for a while, not knowing what to do with it. He didn't care to throw it away. He thought of burning it—respectfully burning it, as one would an old, out-dated, or perhaps defective flag. In the end, he rolled it up gently, carried it out to the garage, and put it in the trunk of the car with the little model of the new cathedral.
>
> The next morning, he noticed that the cross was still there, in outline, on the wall, and that same morning he received word that he was getting an auxiliary bishop—something he certainly hadn't asked for and didn't want—and that the man chosen for the job was Monsignor, or Bishop-elect, Gau.

However, even a correct statement of the abstract meaning of the experience Powers has rendered in the story would be inadequate for revealing its artistic value. Father Kirvan—no doubt inadvertently—underlines Powers' own conviction that a "writer must be 'disloyal' to his religion,"[40] when he upgrades the message of the story at the expense of its artistry: "At this stage of his development," says Father Kirvan, "Mr. Powers is capable of a good deal more than a pleasant rehearsal of a shift in power *whose only* meaning is the delineation of characters." It is, of course, no cause for amazement that a theologically oriented critic should find the "delineation of character" less valuable than the abstract idea.

Yet the theologians must not be permitted to kidnap the fiction of J. F. Powers. Other Catholic writers have faced the same danger, and the successful ones have always resisted. François Mauriac said, "I try to render the Catholic universe of evil in terms of sight, touch, and smell. The sinner about whom the theologian gives us an abstract idea, I make incarnate."[41] And, more recently, Flannery O'Connor expressed the same idea in advising a nun against writing "pious stuff": "I think the first thing you need to realize about fiction is that what the writer does when he writes a story is to try to see an action, or a series of actions, clearly. The key word is *see.*"[42]

XI *Realism and Faith*

The important thing about "Keystone"—and about all of Powers' successful fiction—is that it presents a palpable world, inhabited by complex and emotionally charged human beings confronting their problems. However much those problems may be analogues of the most profound spiritual conflicts faced by modern man, they are manifested in the humble and realistic terms of everyday life—checking the spelling of a word, keeping an eye on the beer stand, or mowing the cemetery lawn. Herein lies the genius of J. F. Powers: the immensity of his understatements. John P. Sisk divides Powers' short stories into two categories: those that are in *the modern realistic tradition* in which commitment to otherworldly values is observed

> with humor, irony, even sympathy, but not with acceptance. Stories like "Prince of Darkness," "The Valiant Woman," "The Lord's Day," and "The Devil Was the Joker," for instance, have coherence and meaning for this kind of realism, even if there is something left over in them it cannot reach. But stories like "Zeal," "Lions, Harts, Leaping Does," . . . and "The Presence of Grace" are another matter. Unless a great deal in them can be written off as the vagaries the artist should be allowed (as Marx allowed them to Heine), or be made the subject of an

athletic or temporary suspension of disbelief, they will be marked down the way we all tend to mark down *stories that offend our sense of reality.* . . . Powers, in short, may bother many of his fellow Catholics because he is too realistic, but he bothers many outside the fold because he is not realistic enough. Conclusive proof of an unresolved conflict in his work may satisfy both parties, but for different reasons.[43]

This kind of subjective, imprecise categorizing will not help to understand Powers' fiction. Even Sisk dimly senses that Powers' standard of judgment in *all* these stories is the same, for he concedes that even in the so-called realistic stories "there is something left over . . . it [realism] cannot reach." Actually Sisk's categories seem to be based on whether or not the central character achieves a saving recognition of his own moral condition and not on the standard by which the moral condition is to be judged.

In the earlier stories Powers generally depicts with hard irony instances of moral failure, and in the later ones he portrays with subtle humor instances of moral success. But there is no inconsistency or unresolved conflict in his value system. If anything, the inconsistency is in the critic. For example, Sisk says of "The Devil Was the Joker" that "Miles [sic], the unarmed innocent in this story, develops armor in his relations with Mac. Mac is a necessary part of his growing up, which in Powers' fiction is a necessary and a good thing."[44] True, but "The Devil Was the Joker" is then in the same class of stories as "Zeal" and "The Presence of Grace," in which the morally deformed serve to prod the protagonist into acquiring moral armor.

As for realism, *all* of Powers' fiction (with the possible exception of the two cat stories) is in the most important sense realistic in that it evokes images of the kind of character and events that can and do occur in cities, slums, suburbs, and in rectories. In fact, a reviewer in the Catholic journal *Renascence* made the error of asserting that " 'The Presence of Grace' does not contain a single problem which is fundamentally spiritual . . . its complexity and seriousness are focused on man-to-man rather than man-to-God relations."[45] Another non-Catholic reviewer has said that "Powers takes the Catholic hierarchy as a world where faith is no issue and makes capital use of that world for fictional invention . . . [all the characters] are hungry for ego-recognition, but have to subdue their hunger to manners."[46]

Such is Powers' skill that any reader whose perceptions are strictly limited to a realistic frame of reference will not feel the absence of any element necessary to a meaningful and coherent whole. But even when a Powers story does not *explicitly* present man-to-God relations, the man-to-man relations always call for some judgment; and the standards of judgment—almost always implicitly invoked—are invariably spiritual. Not to see this quality is very much like observing a high mass as an entertainment, an interesting ritual with fascinating psychological and anthropological connotations, but with no real spiritual significance. But if neither ceremony—the mass or a Powers' story—has meaning in spiritual terms to a given reader, he will be gravely deficient in his total comprehension. Readers who do not personally believe in Catholicism must at least see it at work in even the most casual details of a Powers story: Father Burner putting a golf ball into his clerical collar; the priest in "The Lord's Day" casually hanging his unbuttoned collar around his neck; Monsignor Sweeney taking sides with those invoked in "*Damnant quod non intelligunt*"; Mrs. Klein renaming her bakery "The Purity"; Grace damning an innocent woman, or a bishop failing to be aroused by a guilty one. "All problems are at bottom theological," says the protagonist of "Look How the Fish Live"—and in all of Powers fiction the theology is there. It is not dogmatic or mystical, but ascetic, moral, natural, or pastoral.

CHAPTER 4

The Death of Father Urban

MORTE D'URBAN, which Powers began as a short story for the collection of stories in *Prince of Darkness* but which soon outgrew the limited dimensions of that genre, is in many ways a development and fruition of the themes and techniques of the clerical stories. Father Urban is the crack salesman and public relations man of the Order of St. Clement—which figures prominently in "The Devil Was the Joker" and, during most of the novel, he operates in the diocese of Great Plains, where the Right Reverend James Conor is bishop, Father Udovic his assistant, and Monsignor Renton dean of the Cathedral—all are principal characters in "Dawn." While the novel was still in progress, Powers described it to an interviewer:

> The story is about Father Urban being sent to this foundation of the Order in Minnesota. He had been a big-time speaker, a poor man's Fulton Sheen. He was suddenly sent up here to this white elephant, not as the rector, but as one of the boys, one of the three priests. That's my story, what he did there, how he tried to put the place on its feet, how he worked as a common workman—because that was the rector's idea about everything, saving string; the pound-foolish, penny-wise kind of rector. Father Urban is not that kind of man. He's what used to be the Pullman type, now the type with the attaché case, doing lots of good and instilling a feeling in the young men in the novitiate. Father Urban was trying to develop something special for the Clementines. What it was, he was not sure—a kind of opportunism I would say. . . . I thought it would be a nice little nut-brown novel, all kinds of irony.[1]

I *Irony and the Paranoid Perspective*

Father Urban, the erstwhile Harvey Roche, is one of the most fully exposed of the flawed rocks with which the Church is built; and in the swift pace of a year and a half, from the fall of 1957 to the spring of 1959, he undergoes so many experiences and interacts with such a wide range of diverse characters, both secular and religious, that many critics have been unable to see the clear, steadily developed line of the plot. The fact that several chapters first appeared as short stories in various journals has encouraged more than a dozen critics—the majority of the reviewers—to consider *Morte D'Urban* episodic and disunified. No doubt the critics were confused by the fact that the story is told from the point of view of Urban himself, and he is a very distorting medium whose paranoia and cynical irony tend to flatten characters of the three-dimensional world into stereotypes. The tone and the kinds of observed detail shift as his moods and general metamorphosis require.

But it is Father Urban—and not Powers—who reduces to caricature almost all of his fellow priests within and outside the Order of St. Clement. It is possible for the astute reader to peer around the distorting glass that Urban sets in front of him and see instead the "real" personalities of Father Boniface, the Provincial of the Order, a humble man who seeks to use only humble means to lead his flock to salvation; Father Wilfrid, the rector of St. Clement's Hill, a dedicated, hard-working priest whose pretenses at omniscience and optimism are largely deliberate tactics for getting an impossible job done; Father John Kelleher, an unworldly man who takes seriously his religious vows, especially his vow of obedience; and Monsignor James Renton, the most perceptive of them all, as a double-visioned moralist whose values perfectly match the schizoid role of a secular priest who must stand with one foot in heaven and the other on earth. Not that these men are all saints—not at all; but each is a complex personality who, in his own way, is far more suited to the priesthood than the "go-getter" to whom they appear to be merely assorted impediments to progress.

On the other hand, the wealthy secular characters whom Urban seeks to enlist as benefactors of the Order, *are* mere caricatures of human beings whom Urban refuses to see as such. Billy Cosgrove, "hairy of wrist and sunburned" (11),[2] is a satanic beast who enjoys a roaring fireplace and who drives a flaming red convertible; Mrs. Thwaites is an aged queen of the shades who sits enthroned before her two television sets, both of which simultaneously flicker "a dead light, so that [her] face showed up like a photographic negative . . . [while] a humidifier steamed at her feet. . . . The shades were drawn in all the windows and the temperature was equatorial" (145). But Urban insists upon seeing these figures as human and is quite prepared to sell them and others like them indulgences for their sins.

Only when Urban is painfully reminded of his mortality by a blow on the head from the Bishop's golf ball does his vision improve so that he comes to see these simulacra of humanity for what they really are. Then he encounters Sally Thwaites Hopwood, a sensual woman without a trace of religious hypocrisy and with no illusions that a rabat and a collar automatically convert a man into a priest. From her he learns to see himself and the world about him more accurately. But, unfortunately, most readers have by then become so captivated by the old, worldly Urban that they are unable to follow his metamorphosis into genuine piety.

Any story told from a limited, subjective point of view is automatically two stories—the implicit one of characters and events as they "really" are, and the explicit one of characters and events as they are distortedly seen by the central intelligence. Except for well-trained and highly skillful readers, the implicit story requires at least a second reading. Therefore, anyone seeking to summarize the plot of *Morte D'Urban* must either decide which narrative to condense, or else devise a means of treating both simultaneously.

The plot summaries presented by most reviewers suggest that Urban's point of view is irresistibly compelling; but, since Urban does not see his own experience clearly and whole, the résumés inevitably present an episodic and false impression of the details of the plot and of the novel as a whole. The critics' treatment of one detail—the motive of Father Boniface in removing his best man from the Chicago office and sending him to the isolated, decrepit retreat center in Duesterhaus—may serve as an example. Saul Bellow says that Urban is removed "for reasons not clearly understood,"[3] but other reviewers believe that Urban is "banished by a jealous Father Provincial";[4] that the Provincial "lacks vision and is totally unimpressed by Urban's glittering dreams";[5] that "not all of Father Urban's brothers and superiors understand him . . . and Urban is forced to defer to mediocrity";[6] that the Provincial is "a feckless do-nothing"[7] or "slightly stupid."[8] On this issue only one critic, Harvey Curtis Webster, is able to resist the easy, insidious appeal of Urban's point of view and realize that "the Provincial recognizes early in the novel that [Urban] is too proud of himself and sends him to Duesterhaus."[9]

Now how is an issue like this to be settled? How is the reader to know precisely why Urban was sent to Duesterhaus? Only by taking into account the necessary distortions of the narrative medium and seeing the detail in terms of the entire narrative structure. The reader must keep in mind that it is Urban (and not Powers, who, like Joyce, effaces himself) who at the beginning of the novel sees his superiors in strictly negative terms, but whose judgment is biased by his love of material luxuries—fancy cigars, first-class trains, powerful automobiles—and his inordinate pride in his success as a spiritual huckster—"he felt that the authority might have been his if the members of the Order had only known that by electing him Provincial they would not be losing him in the field" (26).

Furthermore, the close of the novel calls for a restrospective view of the opening; and it is significant that, when the humbled and chastened Urban himself becomes Provincial and his paranoid outlook no longer dominates the narrative, "Father Boniface whom many had thought destined for Texas or New Mexico, was still at the Novitiate—teaching" (333). Urban then, too, takes the blame for cutting down the elms without revealing that "Father Boniface, that hard man, had been too soft to order the job done while the trees were in leaf" (333).

An alert reader can remain sufficiently aloof, can hover over the novel with a detached, critical vision and see everything qualified by context and tone, rather than naïvely accept the neurotic narrative view of Urban as definitive. He will not then make the two crucial errors that a majority of the critics did, first, in seeing *Morte D'Urban* as an episodic satire rather than a unified novel and, second, in judging Urban himself as finally an unredeemed failure.

William H. Gass, for example, says that "the formula (of the shock of contradiction—the bingo game going on under the cross) which has served Powers' shorter fiction so well does not lend itself as readily to the longer form. His situations tend to close upon themselves, making the novel a trifle episodic. . . . I cannot imagine a book in which religious feeling would be more conspicuously absent."[10] And Granville Hicks asserts that "the novel is not Powers' *metier*—clumsy . . . episodic . . . There are no dramatic incidents and no large issues."[11] Martin Price finds "a series of nicely composed vignettes. . . . The irony made for genial sketches in the *New Yorker*, but it makes for oppressive coziness when sustained for so long."[12] Most of the critics are more or less in agreement—those that see the unity of the novel fail to see the redemption of Urban; those that see the redemption fail to see the unified novel.

A rare exception is John P. Sisk, for whom "the novel is not simply a gallery of memorable portraits; characters are revealed in action and interaction."[13] It is unfortunate for the general reading public and for most academic critics that his account, and that of two other very astute reviewers, P. Hinchcliffe (*Blackfriars*) and Marie J. Henault (*America*),[14] appeared in Catholic journals of limited circulation. Miss Henault is perhaps the most perceptive and convincing with her argument that "Powers' amusing satire, with its great fun in incidental *reductio ad absurdum* . . . should not prevent us from seeing the fundamental seriousness of *Morte D'Urban.* Carefully employing the devices of the novelist—plot, character, and symbolism—Powers here presents the great theme of individual salvation. The death of Urban is the saving of him."[15]

The very epigraph of the novel should serve as an indication of the ultimate—and gentle—irony of the whole book: "The life of every man is a diary in which he means to write one story, and writes another."[16] Applied to *Morte D'Urban*, James Barrie's remark means roughly that "Father Urban meant to acquire all the worldly means for building himself and the Order of St. Clement into a powerful organ of the Church, but instead gained his own soul in presiding over the liquidation of the Order." In italics, preceding the "Overture," is an excerpt from one of Father Urban's fund-raising speeches, an example of his soft-sell approach, his fake folksiness, his wit and *savoir-faire*. The man's character is revealed in a flash. But the functional purpose of this preface is to orient the reader to the subjective point of view of the novel.

Powers had written the first draft of Urban's story entirely in the first-person; but certain portions, especially toward the end, called for an external perspective (not necessarily the author's, but that of Urban's milieu), and the whole narrative was recast in the third person—with an Urban lens fitted to the camera eye. In the published version, Urban's distorted view of the world persists until the climactic scenes of the novel, which means that most of the narrative is ironic, often in ways that are not apparent on first reading.

Furthermore, the irony is not intermittent and obvious but subtly cumulative. Thus, for example, although the "Overture" *seems* to present the author's judgment of events, the novel as a whole makes it clear that only from Urban's perspective does it appear that "It had been a lucky day for the Order of St. Clement the day Mr. Billy Cosgrove entered the sacristy of a suburban church after Mass and shook the hand of Father Urban" (1). Only Urban, a Simon Peter fishing for rich benefactors, could imagine it as good luck. He had preached in a "high he-who manner" about various figures in history who had relinquished power for the sake of their souls and had concentrated on "Charles of the Holy Roman Empire—it was he who, you might say, owned and operated Europe but who, in the end, desired only the society of monks" (1). What is immediately striking here is the juxtaposition of the commercial idiom ("owned and operated") with the spiritual ("society of monks"), which capsules Urban's own final experience.

II *Removing the Urban Lens*

By inducing the "hairsplitters" at the Novitiate to send Billy three cords of wood for his fireplace, Urban makes friends with that mammon of iniquity who provides new quarters for the Order in return for the medieval annual rent of prayers and three cords of wood. Instead of being rewarded with the fruits of his labor, however, Urban is given the "green banana" by being sent, together with Father John, to the Order's "white elephant," a retreat center in the remote and appropriately-named community of Duesterhaus (House of Gloom). The rector there, Father Wilfrid, who has heard of Urban's propensities for taking over, is determined to retain his leadership; he shouts gleefully as a flock of geese go by, "Hello! Goodbye! See how they follow their leader!" But Urban doesn't get the message; and during the first meeting of the staff he is surly and querulous. Insensitive to the over-all needs and priorities in renovating the decrepit retreat house, he complains about a squirrel in the walls of his room and demands new eaves. Father John quickly tries to forestall a conflict, but Father Wilfrid subtly indicates that he will not abandon his responsibilities nor be intimidated by the big-shot preacher from Chicago: "There's this to be said for squirrels—*little* red squirrels. . . . They're a very courageous little animal. I'm told a little red squirrel, given the chance, will castrate a grey squirrel. . . . I've often wondered what would happen if a *great* red squirrel came around the house. I don't know but what I'd put my money on the little fella" (74).

In suppressed rage at his defeat, Urban withdraws and broods. He recalls his childhood of poverty and estrangement in a southern Illinois town where Catholics were a persecuted minority and where he had suffered misery at the hands of priests and teachers at the Novitiate.[17] But he remembers with satisfaction that they, in turn, had suffered various terrible fates: "He would not say that life had dealt harshly with these people because of their treatment of him. Not a-tall. '*Revenge is mine.*' And rightly so, for all the crimes of men are crimes against Him, and would be seen as such but for ignorance. Nevertheless, in view of these casualties, it was sobering to think what might befall Father Boniface now that he had joined the select little group of people who'd made life unnecessarily difficult for Father Urban, and that Wilf, if he didn't watch himself, would soon be joining the group" (82-83). Perhaps nowhere in the novel is Urban's paranoia and his ironic self-condemnation more apparent.

For forty days, however, Wilf remains a strict, though considerate taskmaster—exposing Urban's fakery, prodding him into scraping wallpaper, sanding floors, laying on paint, but insisting that Urban wear his oversized cap to protect his hair from arsenic. To Urban this seems "the most difficult period in his life to date" (85). Sullen and resentful, he imagines how the job might be done more easily, but says nothing. "Malice might play a part in such an attitude—a desire to see the ship go down with all aboard, himself included—but wasn't it, except for that, the right attitude for one in his position?" (94).

The Christmas season brings a truce. Wilf submits graciously when Urban replaces his plastic Christmas tree with a seven-foot balsam, and Urban in turn submits graciously to losing regularly at checkers to Jack—"Poor Jack. Of course, his spiritual life was good" (104). But tensions develop when it is discovered that the Christ-child is missing from the electronic nativity crib that Billy Cosgrove had sent to Duesterhaus. Wilf confesses to having removed it because "*He's not born yet*!" (108). Urban's silent fury crackles in the atmosphere until Jack gently reminds Wilf that, by such logic, the shepherds, Mary and Joseph, and the Magi wouldn't be there either. When Wilf concedes the point and restores the Christ-child, his apology, "Just shows how wrong we can be sometimes," makes Urban's gorge rise at the "we." However, seeing a winning move at the checkerboard, he releases his anger there before he realizes that Jack had obviously arranged for him to win. It is one of his rare moments of insight into the charity of others. Humbled by this lesson in the true spirit of Christmas, he says to all, "Let's open one of Billy's bottles" (111).

But that spirit doesn't last. When Wilf refuses Urban permission to replace a vacationing pastor at St. Monica's Church, Urban begins to slack on the job. "Father Urban wondered if [Wilf] might not be acting under instructions from Chicago to keep the star of the Order blacked out" (117). Though it is Christmas, Wilf has no thought of the star of Bethlehem. Alarmed at the expense incurred by Urban's private electric heater, he finally capitulates and sends him to St. Monica's. After forty lean days, Urban is about to have forty fat ones.

A leader once again, Urban becomes dynamic. Despite the protest of Monsignor Rentor that "the fuss would kill him," Urban persuades the ailing pastor, Father Phil Smith, to build a new church and a new wing on the school; and, after Phil leaves for his vacation, Urban plunges vigorously into taking a census of the parish. St. Monica's becomes a "busy, happy rectory. . . .

By the power of his example, and, of course, by God's grace, Father Urban had caused Johnny [Father Chumley, the curate too much concerned with the contemplative life] to question *not* the lives of the saints but his own life as a parish priest" and shaped him into a man of action—though "he was no Father Urban and never would be" (157-61).

When word comes that Father Phil had died while playing golf in the Bahamas, Urban's first thought is of his own chances for becoming the new pastor. His fame as an orator leads him to be assigned the funeral sermon, which he delivers with his usual skill, earning the praise of the Bishop "in the hearing of several mastodons who stood high in the diocese" (179). And when he discovers that the Bishop is really the one who had instigated the building program at St. Monica's, he is emboldened to violate protocol by seeking an interview—a brazen act that costs him the post. The Bishop ironically offers him three remote Indian missions, which, had he been a true priest of the order of Melchizedek, would have seemed a real challenge to him.

Meanwhile, retreatants have flocked to St. Clement's Hill, a phenomenon for which Urban takes all the credit: "The Clementines . . . had got nowhere until Father Urban entered the lists" (188). But, when the departing retreatants fail to leave sufficient tokens of their gratitude, Urban—to whom "the Irish, ecclesiastically speaking, were the master race"—attributes it to "too many Teutonic and Central European strains" and says so to Father Wilfrid Bestudik, whose only response is "Maybe we shouldn't look at it . . . so materialistically" (189).

Quite by chance, Urban discovers that the land adjoining the Hill is for sale, sees an opportunity for drawing a "better class" of retreatants, and arranges for Billy Cosgrove to present the land to the Order for development as a golf course. Sent as emissary to win the approval of the authorities in Chicago, Urban "walks and talks" with even "the dim bulbs whose existence he'd always tried to overlook in the past" (197); and he makes a plea for the prospective retreatant who "would feel funny . . . at, say, a Trappist monastery. . . . Golf was just one way (a good one, Father Urban thought) to get at the problem" (199).

While the golf course is being laid out, Urban serves as the Hill's roving ambassador of good will, often traveling in a sports car borrowed from one of his women admirers. Alerted by Monsignor Renton that the Bishop is considering taking over St. Clement's Hill as a site for a seminary, Urban forgets the advice he had given one of his parishioners—"it never pays to buck a Bishop in his own see." Urban sees himself as the shining knight of the Order about to engage in an ordeal by combat on the golf links. On the ninth hole Urban is in the lead; but, while scanning the wrong portion of the sky, he is struck in the head by the Bishop's ball. One might say that he has always been scanning the wrong portion of the sky, but now he undergoes a symbolic death and rebirth.

In the hospital, upon regaining consciousness after receiving Extreme Unction, Urban overhears Monsignor Renton describe the accident as "an act of God" which saved the Hill for the Clementines. But Urban finds the comment "heretical in its implications, since it made short work of him as a responsible agent of God's will in an orderly universe" (252). He does not immediately become a new man. Instead, he undergoes three trials in which the ironies of the novel are reversed; in each he suffers a secular defeat which is at the same time a spiritual victory.

The first of his trials occurs at the estate of the wealthy Mrs. Thwaites, where he goes to convalesce and to renew his campaign for her good will toward the Order. There he envisages himself a medieval confessor to an apostate queen, but he learns that Monsignor Renton was right when he said that "God is not mocked" by her religious hypocrisy.[18] For Mrs. Thwaites cuts him dead after he attempts to intervene with her on behalf of the Irish maid Katie, a "damsel in distress" who had lost all her savings to Mrs. Thwaites at dominoes.

His second trial comes a month later when the imperious Billy Cosgrove summons him on a fishing trip. "Two days and nights of close association with Billy had left Father Urban feeling anything but complacent about their relationship. More had to be done for Billy in a spiritual way than Father Urban had been doing" (283). Still he avoids a showdown—"Pius IX, who had begun so well, had thrown down his cards in a fit of self-righteousness, and the Church was still trying to get back in the game." Better to operate with finesse, like Lanfranc who "had got William and Matilda to found two abbeys by way of penance for their contumacy" (286). Nevertheless, when Billy after several days without catching a fish (Urban makes the only catch, a two-pound walleye) releases his frustration by attempting to drown a swimming deer, Urban accelerates the boat's engine—and dunks Billy. The irate Billy then throws Urban into the water and abandons him. Forced to swim ashore, Urban finds that Billy has left the resort without paying the bill; he has also taken the station wagon which he had earlier given to the Order.

On his way back to the Hill, the dishevelled Urban is picked up by Sally Thwaites Hopwood, the attractive apostate daughter of his erstwhile benefactress. Having been tempted by the world and the devil, he now faces temptation by the flesh. Sally takes him to her island tower where, drink in hand, he rests by the fire and has a fantasy of himself as he might have been had he not entered the priesthood—a married, successful, world-traveled man of affairs. Sally rouses him with a demand that they go for a swim, and when he refuses she attempts to lure him by exhibiting herself in the nude. The temptation is great, but he resists. Furious at being spurned, she flings her golden-calf shoes at his head and rushes out to drive away in the launch, leaving him to swim ashore for the second time that day.

When he at last returns to the Hill from his abortive fishing trip, he discovers that in his absence his fellow priests had caught seventy pounds of fish in their own lake—"including one wall-eye, an eight pound lunker" (312). While attempting to sweat out his cold by hard work in the garden, Urban swoons. During his second convalescence, he helps Father John transform Malory into an exemplary moral tale ending with Launcelot inducting his fellow knights into Holy Orders.

Leaner and grayer, still suffering from headaches, Urban submits to a Mayo Clinic check-up that reveals no physiological abnormalities. During the next conference at the Hill, the chastened Urban protests nothing, neither the mice in the walls nor the silly intelligence test that Wilf concocts for the Clementine booth at the Catholic Fair. Urban then learns that he has been elected new Provincial of the Order, and he undergoes the ritual in which it is invoked that "in the event . . . that you are depressed by the flesh, a prisoner to sin, blinded by ignorance, in bondage to creatures and things, let us pray . . . that you be gently purged, ardently moved, and made merciful." However, much to the consternation of those who voted for him, Urban proves to be a Provincial strangely indifferent to the Order's worldly fortunes; he gains a reputation for piety "not entirely unwarranted," and "oddly enough, although for many years he'd traveled out of Chicago, he seemed to think of the Hill as home."

Thus drained of the distorting perspective of Father Urban's hilarious wit and the rich evocative details, the plot can be seen as the experience of a man who uses the priesthood as an instrument for worldly success until a traumatic event shocks him into awareness that compromise with the mammon of iniquity is morally and spiritually degrading. Then, as his mortal self declines, he gradually sets his own soul in order, without false piety and even without conscious deliberation. Thus, *Morte D'Urban* is neither "pure satire,"[19] nor "an ironic study of Church politics,"[20] nor "thin on spiritual quality,"[21] nor a delineation of "futility."[22]

III *The Priest Promoter*

Nor is it true that the novel shifts in its formal development and technique, though, of course, the metamorphosis of the central character requires a turning point in the action. But there is more than one turning point. The opening section of the novel has a cyclical movement which is inversely recapitulated in the final section. After his initial success in securing the greatest financial benefactor that the Order of St. Clement has ever had, Urban is sent to the House of Gloom—in worldly terms, a fall; and he sinks to the nadir of his power and pride within the Church (to Chapter Four). Then he begins to rise again, bringing new prosperity to the Order and renewed activity and growth to the parish of St. Monica's; it almost appears that under his aegis the Church might become as successful and efficient an institution as Standard Oil (to Chapter Nine).

But even though twenty-four hours in a strange diocese reveal how desperately the Church needs to succeed in other terms—morally and spiritually—Urban is not yet ready to do combat in those terms; instead he takes on the Bishop's champion in an ordeal by golf. His ambiguous victory-in-defeat in that combat was not an act of his free will, which—as Urban himself indicates—must be the basis of true victory. Nevertheless, it serves as a catapult for the reverse movement. In the ensuing three trials he *is* a "responsible agent of God's will in an orderly universe," and as such can no longer remain blind to the moral consequences of making deals with the mammon of iniquity.

Chapter Twelve is thus the major transition point in a sequence of turns, and not a wrenching of the novel's structure as some critics have suggested. In the final five chapters, the cyclical movement of the first two-thirds of the novel is repeated and inversed: there is a fall in Urban's worldly status outside the Church that is simultaneous with a rise in spiritual quality that culminates in his election. In these chapters the irony modulates from astringent wit directed against Urban to a gentle dramatic irony that registers his newly-won and unselfconscious state of grace. His final failure as Provincial is his greatest victory: he that loseth his Church's worldly life shall find its spiritual life, for what is a man profited, if he shall gain the whole world for his Church, and lose his own soul? Briefly sketched, such is the dynamic structural pattern of the plot of *Morte D'Urban* and its ultimate meaning.

However, within these unifying broad movements, there are other devices that tie the elements of the novel togther into a unified whole. For example, Urban is not arbitrarily remade into a new character; in the end, he is the same man he was in the beginning, but purged of his paranoid aggressions and strengthened in the spiritual qualities which were clearly though faintly manifested in the beginning. The title of the novel aptly labels the central action—it is the worldliness of Urban that dies. Early in the novel, when Billy's chauffeur fulminates at a pedestrian who stands up for his rights against Billy's Rolls Royce, Father Urban "rather admires the pedestrian for standing up to Paul and the Rolls—after all, *they* had started it. . . . Billy made just such demands on him—demands that couldn't quite be met in conscience" (23). In his resentment at being transferred to Duesterhaus, Urban protests against Jack's simple acceptance of religious authority: "Ours not to reason why, is that it?"

> Jack, it seemed, had something to say, but didn't care to say it and was giving the world [i.e., Urban] every possible chance to end first. "No, Urban, it's *not* for us to say, and you know

> it. Not in a thing like this." Jack had spoken with surprising firmness for him . . . [and his] attitude was the right one, of course. (31)

Later, when Jack greets Urban at Duesterhaus without being aware that his brother priest has also been transferred, Urban assumes that Jack's silence is motivated by compassion. Like Didymus with Brother Titus, he attributes qualities of piety to another, even when there is no ground in fact for doing so. And Urban is equally quick to learn a lesson in humility from Jack after the episode of the Christmas tree. "For a moment they had all been lifted up, and this was Jack's way of letting them down to earth, where they had to live." Even at the height of his resentment against Father Wilfrid, Urban is able to recognize that "Wilf was doing pretty well as a workman" (126). And while Urban is at St. Monica's, even though it is Father Chumley's turn to take early morning calls, "Father Urban . . . took a call at three in the morning. Making no attempt to rouse the curate, he went out and anointed a parishioner. He would've said nothing about it. Mrs. Burns heard him go out, though, and spoke to Father Chumley in the morning. . . . 'Forget it,' said Father Urban . . . 'I was happy to go out. I really was. It made me feel like a priest—for a change'" (156).

Thus, a subsurface line of continuity is established which makes it not surprising that, while recuperating from the blow of the Bishop's golf ball, he should feign prolonged incapacity so that Mrs. Thwaites' maid will have to drive him to church and thus gain access to the sacraments (258). To be sure, these are by no means the typical actions of Father Urban in the opening sections of the novel, but they clearly show that he does have the makings of a true priest within him. Hence, it is credible that, when he is purged of the forces that inhibit his spiritual development, he should become indeed the humble and even saintly figure that he is in the end.

This development of a spiritual line of action is paralleled by a sexual one.[23] Sally Thwaites Hopwood's attempted seduction of Father Urban comes as no abrupt intrusion or unrelated episodic event; it is carefully prepared for by a gradual accumulation of sexually charged details, beginning perhaps with Father Urban's night drive to St. Monica's when he has a vision of "some white rabbits playing in a field. Father Urban hadn't realized that rabbits had such fun" (174). Later he worries about the possibly erotic motives for Sylvia Bean's friendliness in lending him her sports car. She asks him to read a stanza from Yeats's "Prayer for my Daughter," which refers to "the loveliest woman born/Out of the mouth of Plenty's horn":

> But Father Urban, with and without benefit of poetry, had been through this sort of thing with too many women . . . and he was afraid Sylvia might be building herself up for a letdown. . . . In effect, by asking him to read the poem, she had put words in his mouth, words he might think but would never speak. . . . And "Loveliest woman born" was pushing it some in her case. "Damned attractive redhead" would've been more like it. Experience had shown Father Urban that a handsome priest couldn't be too careful with women. (219)

His relationship with her terminates rather abruptly after Sylvia takes him to her husband's farm to observe the breeding of a mare. "Much to his surprise, Sylvia got right into the act, so to speak. The last Father Urban heard (for he went off to have a look at the ducks) Sylvia was crying encouragement to the stallion and being cross with the mare" (264).

At Henn's Haven when he is introduced to the young second Mrs. Henn, Father Urban finds her "so attractive that [he] was relieved when she left them for the kitchen. Her scent remained, however. Father Urban moved away from it" (273). But Father Urban cannot escape heterosexual involvements so easily, and he finds himself "discussing the course at the Hill with Mrs. Inglis, a golfer, and not a bad-looking woman. . . . Father Urban had pulled out of the conversation with Mrs. Inglis after she said she was going to tell him a secret if she wasn't careful" (282). Thus, by the time Sally Hopwood, the mahogany-haired temptress whom F. W. Dupee cites as the Guinevere to Urban's Lancelot,[24] seeks to seduce him, the general pattern of attraction and rejection has been well established:

> "You could get a cramp, in your condition, and drown."
> "Wouldn't you save me?"
> . . . "We'd both drown. What a way to go." (306)

There is an ironic undercurrent in this dialogue, generated by the double and triple meanings; and Urban's spiritual victory is enhanced by the fact that, unlike Father Didymus of "Lions, Harts, Leaping Does," he is a virile and aware man in a situation charged with sexual energy.

Apart from the carefully developed lines of spiritual and sexual plot development, the unifying force of Father Urban's experiences is shown also in his vacillations, hypocrisies, and final acceptance of St. Clement's Hill as "home." The various choices open to him are symbolized in his escutcheon (which will be examined in detail shortly) that bears on the left the towering skyscrapers of Chicago and on the right the lofty pines of Minnesota. As his name implies, Father Urban is a city man attracted to sleek automobiles and the pleasures of fine restaurants such as L'Aiglon and the Pump Room. During his first speaking engagement while at the Hill, he hypocritically denies his urban identity: "For many years, I traveled out of Chicago, but now . . . I'm stationed right here in Minnesota—and *very* happy to be here, let me say" (98). But to the Bishop of Great Plains, a Chicago man, he proudly asserts that he still thinks of Chicago as home (185).

Then, while visiting the Zimmermans in Ostergothenburg he tells the wealthy provincials, "I consider Minnesota my home now—and consider myself fortunate" (123). However, in his secular revery at Bellisle, he imagines himself as a successful financier who "for many years . . . traveled out of Chicago, and I'm proud to call it my home" (305). Clearly the skyscrapers and the pines represent opposite poles between which Urban vacillates. When at the end of the novel, Urban is finally purged of his big-city values, he is redeemed: "Oddly enough, although for many years he'd traveled out of Chicago, he seemed to think of the Hill as home" (336)—and the Hill, of course, connotes Christ's Calvary.

IV *Medieval Leitmotifs*

The consistent development of Urban's character is no doubt the dominant unifying force of the novel, but other elements also serve to inter-relate the various parts. Certain leitmotifs appear at various intervals, most of them succinctly presented in Father Urban's coat of arms that was conceived by Powers himself and reproduced on the title page of the novel.

At the very top there is a stag, which in the scene where Billy Cosgrove visits the chapel at the Hill is identified in Brother Harold's mural: "Father Urban explained that this—a stag drinking from three wiggly lines[25]—was known as 'The Living Waters' and symbolized not only baptism but the other sacraments, and therefore, you might say, the Church" (270). Thus, later, the meaning of Urban's saving the deer from being drowned by Billy is perfectly clear. And it is also obvious why the stag appears superior to the knight's helmet on the coat of arms. The helmet—with the lake, the tower, and the hand pointing upwards—refers to one of the important motifs of the novel: the parallel between medieval and modern relations between the Church and the secular world.

The early desert fathers sought to keep their Christianity pure by withdrawing from society, but in the early Middle Ages the clergy were instructed to serve the interests of the Church Militant, and, in fact, separation from the Church Militant came to be regarded as schismatic and the rejection of its apostolic injunctions, as enunciated by St. Irenaeus, as heretical.[26] In its growth as the major force in Western civilization, the Church inevitably found itself involved in ironical paradoxes which have continued to this day and which constitute the major focus of Powers' fiction. The juxtaposition of the stag and the helmet on Father Urban's coat of arms is an appropriate symbol of that paradox.

Beginning with Father Urban's sermon on the first page, the medieval motifs in one form or another pervade the entire novel. Sometimes they assume a rather subtle form, as when the previous tenants of the Order's new quarters in the near North Side are said to be "Panache, Ltd!" (15), a phonograph record firm which, we learn later (280), was evicted by Billy after it had refused to locate some Little Jack Little records for him. The eviction made it possible for the Clementines "to accept Billy's rather medieval terms" for rental of the property. More than once, Urban sees his relationship with Billy in medieval terms: "Some of the most powerful figures in history had been spoiled children like Billy, but humble monks had brought them to their knees and turned their bloody hands to the service of God" (23-24). Even at the very last moment of their relationship, Urban imagines himself a Lanfranc bringing William the Conqueror around as "a considerate and respectful son of the Church" (287).

With his other wealthy benefactor, Mrs. Thwaites, Father Urban has a similar rationale. While boating with her past Belleisle (a name which "probably came from some romantic tale"[27]), Father Urban "listening as to a royal complaint, had a vision of life in late medieval times, when nothing and nobody was for sure, when kings and prelates were selling out right and left" (257). Later, in approaching Mrs. Thwaites on behalf of the pathetic maid Katie, Urban ironically says, "I've just met a damsel in distress" (259).

The helmet on the coat of arms conjures up, in a general way, visions of medieval life. But the title, *Morte D'Urban*, seems to refer more specifically to Malory's tales of King Arthur and the Knights of the Round Table, and it has stimulated a variety of responses from the critics. One rather vague comment is that of John P. Sisk: "the reader needs no special exegesis to see that Father Urban is a man who has gone a strange journey on which he has encountered formidable antagonists, enchantresses, and frightful monsters in faery places."[28] Lucy Johnson is a bit more specific in citing "a tournament of champions on a golf course, where a mortal wound is delivered by the Bishop. There is a momentous sea-fight in which dunkings are exchanged on a fishing trip. There is even a Lady of the Lake, who leaves Urban stranded on an island. And finally, he is a purified Arthur, doing what he must, presiding over the liquidation of his Round Table."[29] This last element, however, strikes J. G. Murray as an unresolved ambiguity: "The *morte* of Arthur, in Malory's version at least, was sad, but somehow noble, or at least fitting and satisfying. But the morte of Urban was his election as Father Provincial. . . . Is he a winner (the motto of the Order is "Be a Winner") or loser? . . . It is a Puzzle."[30]

More perceptive readers have seen that "apparently Urban is *not* meant to be Arthur, but Lancelot, the worldliest and most sinful knight redeemed as the most pious hermit and true priest,"[31] even though another reviewer insists that "as Sir Lancelot, Urban is hopelessly miscast."[32] It may be that the "Arthurian myth structure" of *Morte D'Urban* is "almost impenetrable"[33] and that "sooner or later someone will have to write a Ph.D. dissertation to examine the connection between *Morte D'Urban* and *Morte D'Arthur.*"[34] Yet a step in the right direction was taken by Thomas Curley, whose brief comment is that "ironic literature, Professor Northrop Frye points out, begins with realism and tends toward myth. . . . Throughout the last hundred pages Powers has parodied the patterns of Arthurian romance. Father Urban suffers, and suffers deservedly, but he endures and, in a sense, prevails. It may be paradoxical, but in tending toward the myth by way of parody, Urban grows in humanity."[35]

The Arthurian matter is obviously embedded in the novel so realistically that it seems a natural part of an ongoing plot development, but it nevertheless endows the action with a larger significance. Yet it does so by inversion. A careful observer will notice that the helmet in Urban's escutcheon has a large dent in it, which lends credence to Marie Henault's very astute observation that, "like Joyce with his Homeric material in *Ulysses,* Powers reinvents comically verbal bits from the chivalric legends." Father Urban "enters the lists," is said to have his "ordeal by combat," tries to rescue a "damsel in distress," has his knightly "swoon," at one time holds a sword (a tiny, ineffectual letter opener). Lakes figure largely in the action, too, and a launch (an Arthurian barge). In the final chapter, Father John discusses at length his rewriting of the Lancelot story.[36]

Most importantly, however, Powers seems to be using the legend to elevate Father Urban into a figure of more heroic stature than he would be in a straight realistic narrative. Like Lancelot, Urban first chooses the earthly road instead of the heavenly and thus fails to find the Grail (sanctity). But having weathered his temptations, again like Lancelot, he can through three trials, occurring on or near lakes, at last achieve salvation. Thus, it is not true that "the Malory echoes are meant to provide only grace notes to the comic tune of the Novel," as F. W. Dupee believes.[37] Miss Henault's comparison of Powers' use of Malory with Joyce's use of Homer is a brilliant insight which is confirmed by close analysis, despite Powers' own disclaimer that all he "wanted was the way Lancelot changed from the most famous knight, the most excellent knight, to a monk and a priest."[38]

The mere fact of parallel transformations does not in itself explain enough, because the means of transformation must be accounted for: the inversion of the medieval romances. In the medieval tradition the knight worships and desires the unattainable lady from afar until he proves himself worthy of the privilege of making love to her; then the earthly love dissolves as the knight moves on to the higher love of God. But Powers, like Father John in the novel, inverts his source—though in a more sophisticated manner. His knight is already a man of holy orders, and he is pursued by a lady who clearly recognizes the unworthiness of the "operator" behind the priestly façade. It is in rejecting her, despite the temptation, that he becomes worthy of a higher love. In any case, the important point here is that the ironic medieval references begin to accumulate force very early in the novel and serve, together with other techniques, to unify the whole work.

There remain two devices on Urban's escutcheon that call for comment—the fish and the motto, "Be a Winner." The fish, of course, is the traditional symbol of Christ, which, though never explicitly invoked as such in the novel, is frequently employed as an embedded and often ironic symbol. On the door of the Clementines' Chicago Loop offices still appear the titles of the former tenants, publishers of erotic books, among whom is one "Dr. Fish."[39] While enmeshed in the urban world, neither Urban nor the Clementines can be very effective servants of the departed Christ; but at St. Clement's Hill in Duesterhaus, the poverty of the monks requires that they eat fish as a steady diet. Even when it is succulently prepared by the pious Brother Harold, Urban—who prefers sheesh-kebab and champagne—chafes at it and is delighted to have the opportunity of a "real meal" when invited to dine with Mr. and Mrs. Bean. But the most dramatic use of the symbol occurs during Urban's fishing trip with Billy Cosgrove. So far removed from Christ is Billy that he cannot catch a single fish, and Urban himself catches only a two-pound walleye which he must throw back into the lake. Upon his return to the Hill, Urban discovers that Brother Harold has frozen over seventy pounds of fish taken from Holy Spirit Lake.

The legend on Urban's coat of arms, which reads, "Be a Winner," connotes values of the world of business and athletics; it is, therefore, an ironic contrast with the religious mottoes usually borne by the medieval knights. It is further ironic that Father Urban got it from his mentor Father Placidus, who inducted Harvey Roche into the priesthood by revealing to him that religion "need not always be little Tarcisius with the Blessed Sacrament concealed in his breast, pursued by government troops" (79). Although Urban admonishes the curates in St. Paul that "it was not required that they succeed, but only that they do their best" (37) and later prods Father Smith into building a new church with the injunction, "At least a man can try. Sometimes that's the most a man can do" (153), he thinks of himself as a man who wins: "They loved a winner. It was as simple as that" (188). For this reason he cannot submit obediently to the Bishop, but feels obliged to take on the Bishop's champion in combat: "*Be a Winner! Never say die!*" (246). Yet, as he learns, a priest's victory can only come in defeat and in the manner of his dying—when he surrenders passion to regret.

As the noble lines from St. Bernard of Clairvaux put it, the blessed shall achieve their victory in coming to see God "by the toil of humility, by the emotion of compassion, by the ecstasy of contemplation" (329). For Powers himself this idea has become an article of faith, and it is a dominant theme in his entire body of work. As he said in an interview with Sister Kristin, "You can't be a winner, but you can go down like a winner. No one is going to miss death, but you can live and you can die well. . . . It is in line with the facts of life. Certainly with the Church."[40] Hence, the irony of Urban's motto involves a second involution—it proves to be true because Urban becomes a winner in the highest sense by losing.

V *The Mammon of Iniquity*

Urban's original desire was to become a winner by finding "the time and the energy to make friends, as enjoined by Scripture, with the mammon of iniquity" (20), an obvious reference to Luke XVI:1-9, which is another of the recurrent motifs that unify *Morte D'Urban.* In that parable, according to the Douay version, the lesser lord commends his unjust steward: "Make unto you friends with the mammon of iniquity, that when you shall fail, they may receive you into everlasting dwellings. . . . If then you have not been faithful in the unjust mammon; who then will trust you with that which is the true?" This concept is dramatically at work in all of Urban's secular relationships until his conversion by golf ball, and it is implicitly attacked—especially in the first scene with Mrs. Thwaites—by Monsignor Renton, who is "a norm against which the deviation of the main character can be measured."[41] Renton knows that Mrs. Thwaites is a fake Christian and that God is not mocked by the riches which she bestows upon the Church. To deal with her in any way except "in administering the sacraments, was just time wasted for a priest" (149).

Yet Urban persists in his time-serving and even arranges for a holy golf course at St. Clement's Hill for the likes of Billy Cosgrove. However, as Professor G. B. Caird of Oxford points out, "the parable of the dishonest steward bristles with difficulties which have given rise to a great variety of conjectural interpretations."[42] Those theological conjectures are marvelously parodied in the conversations at Zimmerman's country retreat, where Urban reveals that he frankly does not understand the Biblical text and

> "for some years now, when the Sunday for it rolled around, Father Urban had read it, yes, but had cut back to I Paralipomenon in the Old Testament where you got substantially the same idea (the advisability of using our present situation as a preparation for our next one) in a much more acceptable form. Father Urban's sermon on the financing of the temple—'And they gave for the works of the house of the Lord: of gold, five thousand talents, and ten thousand solids: of silver, ten thousand talents: and of brass, eighteen thousand talents: and of iron, a hundred thousand talents,' and so on—was one of his better jobs." (229)

Urban's kid-glove treatment of the rich is, of course, in the interest of the Church Militant, but it is also in his own personal interest as a man of worldly tastes. Early in the novel it is said of Urban that "as a Clementine, he possessed nothing, and the cassock he wore around the Novitiate was pocketless—St Clement of Blois, the Holy Founder of the Order, having regarded pockets rather than money as the root of evil—but Father Urban was away from the Novitiate most of the time, and while he was away his pockets filled up" (14). Urban's interest in money is in marked contrast with the way Father John loses his wallet in the hilarious episode in which he inadvertently exchanges trousers with Father Chmielewski. Powers has said that the norm of the novel is really a composite of both Father John and Monsignor Renton: "Father John, Jack . . . that's the kind of priest I am very fond of—the really simple man, decent as anything and no fool, though you might think so."[43]

By the end of the novel Urban no longer uses the parable of Luke as a rationalization for money-gathering and approaches the simplicity of Father John. There is, for example, a considerable difference between his first arrival in Duesterhaus, when the surly station agent demands a dime for a phone call to the Hill, and his experience after swimming ashore without shoes at Lake Lucille. There the gas station attendant points to the telephone on the desk, saying, "Use this one . . . it won't cost you," as if to underline the fact that a humble priest in need will always find a good Samaritan who doesn't have to be conned into giving aid to the Church. Inducted as Father Provincial, he can reply with sincerity to the interrogations required in the *Regula S. Clementis necnon Rituale Ordinis Ejus:*

> Rector: Need I speak to you of the dangers in pockets?
> Father Urban: No. Of them I have heard and will them avoid as occasions of sin, though in themselves they are not evil. (327)

Apart from these broad motifs, there are still other devices that attest to the unified conception of the work.

One of the most prominent of these—and one prominent in Powers' fiction since the very beginning and used most effectively in "Look How the Fish Live"—is the use of animal imagery. Powers has confessed to a great fascination with animals—"They're always illustrating some moral fact of life."[44] Apart from the stag and the fish, the novel is full of bees, horses, dogs, cats, squirrels, mice, gophers, hamsters, skunks, turtles, geese, wrens, starlings, doves, wolves, and even gorillas (many of which have been cited with suggestions of their symbolic significance in the plot summary).

In general, the city priest does not get on very well with animals; squirrels keep him awake at the Hill, a hamster wets him while he is taking the census for St. Monica's, the dove refuses to feed from his hand at Lake Lucille. However, the dog is the most recurrent of these animal images. Upon his arrival at the railroad station in Duesterhaus, Urban is eyed suspiciously by an old dog lying behind the counter, and when he leaves, he takes his attaché case with him, "remembering that a dog had once wet on it in Pittsburgh" (40). And at Mirror Lake, while visiting the Zimmermans, Urban is compelled to remove his rabat and collar from the auto seat to make way for Mr. Studley's dog—the same dog that growls menacingly at him when he climbs into the cockpit of "Sir Satan," Mr. Studley's biplane.

Father Wilfrid, however, gets along well with dogs and is delighted to acquire Rex along with the property that is to be developed as a golf course. But even he loses the dog's affection to Jack, who is, of course, the most priestly of the fathers at the Hill. However, the real winner is not necessarily the one who gains the ultimate affection of the beast; like Father Burner in "Defection of a Favorite," Urban never succeeds with animals—but in the end he no longer has to.

VI *Satire and Divine Comedy*

The recurrence of such substantive details serves as a significant unifying force in the novel, but even more powerful is the pervasive comic tone, a characteristic most vividly remembered by readers and most avidly discussed by the critics. Everyone agrees that the novel contains comic elements, but critics are not at all agreed on the quality and purpose of the comedy. Granville Hicks flatly asserts that Powers is "essentially a comic writer,"[45] and Thomas Curley refers to "the gaiety of his wit"[46]; but F. J. Gallagher says that the novel "has been widely misjudged. For all its humor, and whatever may be the intentions of the author, the story of Father Urban is a tragic one."[47]

A more subtle contrast may be seen in the remarks of Edward P. J. Corbett and Phoebe Adams. Corbett says that "admirers of Evelyn Waugh, James Thurber, and Muriel Spark will revel in this book. Here is the same kind of dish—a melange of zany fallible characters . . . and low-keyed ironic humor that can suddenly plunge the reader into spasms of laughter."[48] But Miss Adams says that "*Morte D'Urban* . . . is a sad novel with a wittily amusing manner."[49] Richard Sullivan finds it a "comic novel with some fine slapstick touches . . . witty, alive with bright phrasing,"[50] and Father O'Halloran sees that the "irony is tempered with compassion and sometimes marvelous humor."[51] But the French reviewers, accustomed to a rich comic literary tradition, found *Morte D'Urban* cold: "sec comme le froid d'une matinée d'hiver" and "l'humour de J. F. Powers [est] impersonnel et froid."[52]

Obviously the complex involutions of Powers' comic technique simply baffle some readers. James G. Murray says that Powers "possesses (or is possessed by) a great comic spirit . . . but its Ariel delight and Puckish sprightliness seem somehow deployed, diverted, and otherwise denied. . . . What is funny—the bumbling and bungling, for example—gets involved what simply isn't very funny—a lonely priest, a messed-up vocation."[53] But Hayden Carruth more clearly understands that such a paradox is precisely the requirement of great satire in the classical tradition that stretches from Erasmus to Swift—and perhaps to H. L. Mencken, Ring Lardner, and Sinclair Lewis: "J. F. Powers has written a book which is satire in the pure sense—not a symbolic action in the manner of Joyce or Kafka, not a psychological comedy in the manner of Proust or Faulkner, decidedly not a burlesque morality in the manner of Kingsley Amis or Peter DeVries, though all of these can be turned to critical ends—but a pure satire which will nevertheless please the most sophisticated literary taste."[54]

Most perceptive of all on this issue is Thomas Merton, the Trappist monk and poet, who sees that the satire, though powerful, is not an end in itself; it is gradually modulated to become an instrument serving a larger, more compassionate purpose:

> The epic of Father Urban begins in the usual Powers' style: sustained and withering irony. The first half of the book has an intensity about it that will perhaps discourage those who are

> disposed to mistrust and fear this seemingly cold, perhaps even clinical satire: it has never been so sharp and incisive. But is it really cruel? Is it negative? Those who stay with the book will find a change in attitude in the last chapters, and they will discover that Father Urban has become a sympathetic, in some ways admirable person. The fact is that the "death" of Urban is the death of a superficial self leading to the resurrection of a deeper, more noble, and more spiritual personality. This novel is more than a ribald satire on the clergy. It is a valid and penetrating study of the psychology of a priest in what is essentially a spiritual conflict.[55]

In other words, so long as the comedy maintains an aggressive quality, as it does before the purgation of Urban's worldliness, it can properly be classified as great classical satire. But the comedy of *Morte D'Urban* is initially satiric wit—not humor, but wit—which modulates into humor and finally into a quiet seriousness and even a sombre grandeur at the end. The modulations of the comedy are appropriately concomitant with the metamorphosis of the central character.

Once again, clear understanding of the novel in this respect demands insight into the complex workings of Powers' point-of-view technique. For the satire of the first twelve chapters is involuted and multiple. From the perspective of a worldly observer, Father Urban himself satirizes the foibles of his incompetent fellow priests in the Order of St. Clement; and his sustained and withering irony has so aroused the wrath of certain clerical reviewers that they have misunderstood the novel.[56] But at the same time the detached witness—the author and the competent reader—observes Urban himself as an object of irony. A revealing example may be the dialogue concerning the necessity of wearing long underwear in the house which Wilf is too incompetent to heat:

> That evening [Urban] came to the table sneezing.
>
> "Oh, oh, I was afraid of that," Wilf said. "And I'll bet you're not wearing long underwear."
>
> "No, as a matter of fact, I'm not."
>
> "I knew it. I was the same way once." Wilf said that he'd got over his pride, or whatever it was that kept people from wearing long underwear, and so had Brother Harold. . . .

> Father Urban had run across dedicated wearers of long underwear before. They were very sensitive people who were best humored in their cause, but this wasn't easy to do without seeming to give in to them and it. (58-59)

Most readers are easily seduced into identifying with Father Urban's worldly wit and sophistication and into joining in the sneer at Wilf's paternalistic, know-it-all loquacity concerning woolen underwear. But who comes to the table sneezing? Again and again, in much more serious confrontations concerning obedience to authority, the materialistic evaluations of methods and progress, and religious morality, Father Urban is the victim of his own attitudes and, from the perspective of the detached observer, the real butt of the witticisms. For example, his long day's sufferance of Zimmerman's idiocies—"*Time* magazine is pink!"—ends with his discovery that Zimmerman's son is Father Prosperus, a Dolomite, whose order will undoubtedly receive any largesse to be distributed by that mammon of iniquity.

The terms "victim" and "butt" also suggest that *Morte D'Urban* is, for the most part, vicious satire as in "Prince of Darkness," rather than genial humor as in "The Presence of Grace." Yet, even though most commentators have spoken of the fact that *Morte D'Urban* is a comic novel, not one has observed the crucially important fact that never is Urban—or any other character, for that matter—depicted as laughing! It is the reader who plunges into spasms of laughter, and he laughs *at*, not *with*, the characters.

Nevertheless, the tone of the comedy shifts as the perspective of Urban, the central intelligence, becomes less and less aggressive toward others and more perceptive of his own moral condition. As Herbert McArthur observes in a very astute general discussion of the genres of comedy and tragedy, "Comedy comes not to destroy, but to restore balance. . . . The essential job of comedy is to keep a given system of values in proportion; the comic spirit does not challenge the system but rather calls attention to inconsistencies and lack of proportion within it. . . . not the system itself, but only the relative shaping of it may be questioned."[57] In *Morte D'Urban* the shift from destructive satire to a comedy which restores balance begins at the opening of Chapter Twelve, when Urban is lying in his hospital bed:

> "He's one in a million," said Monsignor Renton.
> "One of our best men," said Wilf.
> "A dazzling performance," said the Bishop, repeating himself.
> Father Urban smiled mushily and broke his silence. "Up to a ploint," he said. (253)

This is one of Powers' most brilliant strokes—Urban's speech defect, coming as the climax of a series of eulogies, has the effect of comic reversal. But, since it is the result of neurophysiological shock and perhaps brain damage, it is also poignant; for the first time Urban is the object of genuine sympathy. To be sure, the characters around Urban continue to engage in their zany antics—especially Billy in his dance-band imitations at Henn's Haven (which for Father Urban is as much a "haven" as St. Clement's Hill has been). But Urban does not again so much as light up another Dunhill Monte Cristo Colorado Maduro No. 1; and he is able to reply with a perceptively sober "You may be right" to Chester Henn's observation that "You and me got the same problem. . . . The cold months. We ought to operate in Florida in the cold months—instead of closing down the way we do" (278).

And when Urban is the victim of another's aggression—as when he is struck in the head with Sally Hopwood's golden calf shoe—he is a completely sympathetic victim in an unambiguously righteous cause—not as when he was struck by the Bishop's golf ball. When Jack's description (from Malory) of Sir Launcelot as a man who took "such abstinence that he waxed full lean" is immediately followed by "'You've lost some weight,' said Mr. O'Hara" (319), Urban's identity as a sympathetic hero is complete. And the genial humor begins to modulate toward the poignant close of the novel. Not that the irony disappears, for it is ironic that Urban achieves his goal of becoming Father Provincial for a purpose other than he intended.

This general interpretation is borne out by Powers' account of his experience in writing *Morte D'Urban:*

> I started this book with a different view of Urban than I ended up with. Father Urban grew on me. When I started the book, I had no such plan for him [as redemption]. . . . But I

> got to care more and more about Urban. . . . It's something I have experienced from the very beginning, probably the first time in "Lions, Harts, Leaping Does." . . . I did, yes [come to have a great compassion for him], although I never really fell down on my knees and got weepy about him. I kept it pretty severe, I think. . . . It is an earned kind of compassion. . . . I think he comes closer to—I was going to say Pope John, but I would not want to say that because he's too far away from that. But still he enters into a kind of philosophy, a kind of acceptance which is not cowardly, which is not weak.[58]

Thus, the conclusion is simply quiet, dramatic irony without a trace of satire left; and the comedy is of the very highest and noblest kind in an even greater tradition than that of Swift and Sinclair Lewis—namely, the comedy of Aeschylus' *Oresteia* which began a line that stretches through Dante's *Divine Comedy* to Joyce's *Finnegans Wake*.[59] Urban's *morte,* in fact, leads to his *wake* in one of the finest novels of modern American literature. In *Morte D'Urban* Powers has achieved the rare combination of the religious spirit with the comic spirit, both of which, as Marie Swabey observes, are metaphysical in that "both intimate what the universe is, that it involves a basic coherence over-reaching passing incoherences, an order superseding disorder, and enveloping cosmos beyond the semblances of chaotic detail." She also says that

> Both include a kind of paradox: the religious consciousness, as Santayana says somewhere, feels that "it is right that things should be wrong, yet it is wrong not to strive to right them," whereas the comic spirit, though it lacks a fervent sense of providential control and moral obligation, is nevertheless torn between delight in the incongruities confronting it everywhere and a sense of challenge to resolve them. . . . While the spirit of the religious man remains submissive, reverential, worshipful of a providential power, that of the comedian remains disobedient, irreverent, and disrespectful.[60]

Though Mrs. Swabey did not have Powers in mind, her juxtaposition of the religious and the comic spirit describes perfectly the sensibility which Powers brought to his short stories and developed to a brilliant climax in *Morte D'Urban.* It is a triumph rare in American literature.

Notes and References

Chapter One

1. Frank O'Connor, "Reflections of a Petty World," *Saturday Review of Literature,* XXXIX (March 24, 1956), 22.

2. The most extended commentary that Powers has made concerning his literary credo was evoked in an interview with Sister M. Kristin Malloy, O.S.B., published in the *American Benedictine Review,* XV (March, 1964), 63-80.

3. Malloy, p. 63.

4. Pete Hamill, "The Art of J. F. Powers," New York *Post Sunday Magazine,* March 24, 1963, p. 10.

5. *Books,* I (January, 1965), 7.

6. New York *Times Book Review,* January 25, 1959, p. 1.

7. Eve Auchincloss and Nancy Lynch, "Disturber of the Peace: James Baldwin." *Mademoiselle,* LVII (May, 1963), 207.

8. Malloy, p. 64.

9. Powers, "Art, the Moon Prince," *Commonweal,* XLVIII (May 14, 1948), 105.

10. Powers, review of Elizabeth Bowen *et al., Why Do I Write?* in *Renascence,* II (Spring, 1950), 169.

11. Powers, "Short and Select," *Commonweal,* L (August 5, 1949), 415-17.

12. Sister M. Bernetta Quinn, O.S.F., "View From a Rock: The Fiction of Flannery O'Connor and J. F. Powers," *Critique,* II (1958), 19.

13. Malloy, p. 74.

14. Letter from editors of *The New Yorker* to Mildred Rust, Brooklyn *Tablet*, July 15, 1950, p. 5.

15. Letter to the author, February 3, 1964.

16. "Short and Select," pp. 415-16.

17. Tom Hutchinson, "Talk with J. F. Powers," *Catholic Messenger,* April 16, 1959, p. 2.

18. Malloy, pp. 63-64, 77-78.

19. Donald McDonald, "Interview with J. F. Powers," *The Critic,* XIX (October-November, 1960), 88.

20. Matthew Hoehn, ed., *Catholic Authors* (Newark, N.J.: 1952), II, 456.

21. Letter to the author, May 18, 1965.

22. McDonald, p. 89.

23. J. F. Powers' first daughter was named Katherine Anne, after Miss Porter.

24. McDonald, p. 90.

25. Powers, "She Stands Alone," *Four Quarters,* XII (November, 1962), 56. Both these writers have reciprocated Powers' high praise. Waugh cites

Powers as "almost unique in his country," and Miss Porter says that Powers has "an extremely conscious mind with a real sense of form." Hoehn, p. 456. In a recent interview, Miss Porter reaffirmed her high estimate: "He has been for a good while a superb artist, so at last one of our prize-winning organizations got round to giving Mr. Powers an award, and high time, too." *Harper's Magazine*, CCXXXI (September, 1965), 67.

26. Malloy, p. 79.

27. "Dealer in Diamonds and Rhinestones," *Commonweal*, XLII (August 10, 1945), 408.

28. Review in *Accent*, V (Summer, 1945), 245.

29. Malloy, p. 67.

30. McDonald, p. 21.

31. Hamill, p. 10.

32. McDonald, p. 21.

33. Bob Lundegaard, "Author: 'Writing is Sweaty Job,'" *Minneapolis Sunday Tribune*, April 7, 1963, Feature Section, p. 1.

34. Hutchinson, p. 2.

35. "Waugh Out West," *Commonweal*, XLVIII (July 16, 1948), 327.

36. *Time*, LXVII (March 19, 1956), 110.

37. Frederick J. Stopp, *Evelyn Waugh* (Boston, 1958), p. 193.

38. *The Crazy Fabric: Essays on Irony* (London, 1965). Cf. also the chapter on "Irony and Satire" in M. C. Swabey, *Comic Laughter* (New Haven, 1961).

39. Malloy, p. 72.

40. J. P. Shannon, "J. F. Powers on the Priesthood," *Catholic World*, CLXXV (1952), 435. With greater perspective and in a different mood, Father Shannon—now Bishop Shannon—says of Father Urban in a letter to the author, December 9, 1964:

> Throughout the greater part of the novel his trials are very similar to those of the rest of us in the priesthood and in administrative jobs. We are trying to be faithful to an original vision and commitment at the same time that we ring doorbells, shake tamborines, and try to raise money for worthy causes. Throughout eighty percent of that novel I saw myself in the shoes of Father Urban very graphically, not to say painfully. . . . I believe that the novel is an affirmative one, that it takes a positive stance on the priesthood, its dignity and its burdens.

41. Hoehn, p. 455.

42. M. L. Holton, "J. F. Powers," *Wilson Library Bulletin*, XXXVIII (September, 1963). 80.

43. McDonald, p. 88.

44. *Morte D'Urban* (New York, 1962). p. 76.

45. Letter to the author, June 20, 1965.

46. McDonald, p. 88. Cf. also Lundegaard, p. 1. Powers' attitude contrasts interestingly with that of James Joyce, who said, "It was not a question of belief. I knew I could not live the life of a celibate." Padraic and Mary Colum, *Our Friend James Joyce* (New York, 1958), p. 206.

47. McDonald, p. 88.

48. Hoehn, p. 455.
49. Hamill, p. 10.
50. "Fun with a Purpose," *Commonweal,* XLVIII (Oct. 15, 1948), 10.
51. Hoehn. p. 455.
52. On April 3, 1943, Powers failed to report for induction and was arrested two weeks later. He spent three days in the Cook County Jail before being released on $1,000 bond. He was then indicted by the grand jury on May 6, 1943, and on June 7 pleaded not guilty. He waived jury trial and on September 20 was sentenced to three years in Sandstone Prison in Minnesota. After serving thirteen months and twenty days of his sentence, he was paroled on November 1. 1944. Cf. "United States of America versus James Farl Powers," United States District Court, Northern District of Illinois, April-November. 1943.

Powers has recently reviewed a socio-historical study of an Austrian peasant, a not very bright or especially saintly man, who endured beheading rather than serve in Hitler's army during World War II. In that review, written almost a quarter-century after his own trial of faith, Powers describes the situation of his Austrian counterpart in a manner which shows that he has not altered his convictions:

> Since Rome has traditionally had nothing to say about the justness or unjustness of war, leaving this to the consciences of the antagonists, few of the faithful now look to the Church for guidance in the matter. And yet the impression remains that war is not beyond the moral jurisdiction of the Church, and could, conceivably, be the subject of censure, like divorce. contraception, and books. Hitler's wars (and Mussolini's African campaign before) show how far the Church can accommodate some of her members, and incidentally herself. That many more people haven't been scandalized by the Church's passivity may show the wisdom of her policy *as policy,* but it also shows what—how little—the Church militant means to most people. It also suggests why this is so.
>
> Nevertheless, Professor Zahn believes that the Church alone among the institutions of society has the potential to counteract the force of the secular authority. What hope he has for the *individual* is in the Church. But since the Church has so often run with the hounds, it is a forlorn hope, really only a wish. . . . What nobody in this book seemed to understand at the time, perhaps not even Jägerstätter [the victim], was that *he* believed in God and the hereafter as others didn't—and could afford to live and die as others couldn't.

Review of Gordon Zahn, *In Solitary Witness: The Life and Death of Franz Jägerstätter, Commentary,* XL (July, 1965), 91-92.

53. Letters from Fr. George Garrelts (November 27, 1964) and Fr. John Hugo (April 26, 1965) to the author. It is simply not true, as Fr. J. P. Shannon charges, that "only by some kind of dissimulation or deceit" could Powers have attended a priests' retreat. Cf. "J. F. Powers on the Priesthood," pp. 435-36.
54. Conversation with the author, November 30, 1964.
55. "Night in the County Jail," *Catholic Worker,* X (May, 1943), 8.

56. "Saint on the Air," *Catholic Worker,* X (December, 1943), 8.
57. Lundegaard, p. 6.
58. *New Yorker,* XXIII (November 15, 1947), 29-33.
59. *New Yorker,* XXV (January 28, 1950), 23-25.
60. Hamill, p. 10.
61. Robert Lowell, "The Art of Poetry," *Paris Review* VII (1961), 73.
62. *New Yorker.* XXVIII (December 13, 1952), 39-41; and *Newman Annual* (1958), 34-42.
63. Powers, Letter to Father George Garrelts, June 5, 1958.
64. Lundegaard, p. 1.
65. Hamill, p. 10.
66. All but the last sentence was printed in the New York *Times Book Review,* May 12, 1963, p. 2.
67. Powers, Letter to Richard Keefe, March 21, 1963.
68. *Kenyon Review,* XXVI (Spring, 1964), 305-16.
69. "Night in the County Jail," p. 8.
70. Powers, "Day in the County Jail," *Catholic Worker,* X (July, 1943), 6-7.
71. "Saint on the Air," p. 8. Cf. also Father John J. Hugo, *Applied Christianity* (privately printed, 1944), pp. 9-10, 32.
72. "Fun with a Purpose," pp. 9-12.
73. Powers, "St. Paul, Home of the Saints," *Partisan Review,* XVI (July, 1949), 714-21.
74. Any playing footloose and fancy-free with the sacrament of marriage, for example, arouses his satiric ire. When one of the cheap men's magazines published an "authentic" account of group copulation among four married couples, Powers responded with a devastating piece in the form of a Christmas letter from one couple to another lamenting the problems of share-and-share-alike materialism. "Are These Our Children?," *The Nation,* CXC (December 10, 1960), 453-54.
75. Powers, "Moonshot," *The Nation,* CXCII (March 3, 1962), 195-96, 204.

Chapter Two

1. Hamill, p. 10.
2. References to Powers' short stories, cited in parentheses, are to *Prince of Darkness* (New York, 1948) and *The Presence of Grace* (New York, 1956), except for the uncollected stories for which see the bibliography below. Of "He Don't Plant Cotton," John Cogley said, "Here Powers does not fall into a trap. . . . There are no types, no walking propaganda blurbs. His Negroes, like his priests, are people. He is reverently careful to respect human personality with all its complexity, inconsistency, uniqueness. His is the method of the mature artist, and his outlook is that of the mature, full-sized Catholic." Review of *Prince of Darkness, Catholic Worker,* XIV (July-August, 1947), 5. Cogley here more accurately characterizes the aims rather than the achievements of Powers' Negro stories, for only in the portrayal of Baby does he begin to approach complexity and depth; otherwise, both Negro and white characters all too conveniently fit stereotypes

of the liberal mind. Perhaps Elisabeth Hardwick is closer to an accurate judgment in her observation that the Negro stories, though they "indicate a good ear for common speech and an ardent devotion to the Negro's cause, . . . suffer from . . . the powerlessness of literature as propaganda." *Partisan Review,* XIV (September-October. 1947), 537.

3. "The Complex Moral Vision of J. F. Powers," *Critique,* II (1958), 36.

4. Quinn, p. 23.

5. Evelyn Waugh, "The Loneliness of Mr. Powers," *Catholic World,* CLXIX (May, 1949), 151.

6. Robert Daniels, review of *Prince of Darkness, Sewanee Review,* LVI (Summer, 1948), 527.

7. McDonald, p. 21.

8. The character is based on Marian Anderson, even though she had not yet sung for Toscanini.

9. Anon., review of *Prince of Darkness, Times Literary Supplement* (London), October 23, 1948, p. 593.

10. Eunice S. Holsaert, "Disciplined Distaste," New York *Times Book Review,* May 4, 1947, p. 20.

11. In a review of *Nabokov's Dozen.*

12. Sisk, p. 39.

13. Donald Barr, "Doors That Open on a World in Little," New York *Times Book Review,* March 18, 1956. p. 5.

14. Quinn, p. 24.

15. Sisk, p. 38.

16. Conversation with the author, Nov. 30, 1964.

17. George Scouffas, "J. F. Powers: On the Vitality of Disorder," *Critique,* II (Fall, 1958), 54.

18. *Ibid.*

Chapter Three

1. Malloy, p. 69.

2. Sister Mariella Gable, O.S.B., *This is Catholic Fiction* (New York, 1948), p. 30.

3. Henry Rago, review of *Prince of Darkness, Commonweal,* XLVI (August 22, 1947), 457.

4. Jack B. Ludwig and Richard Poirier, *Instructor's Manual to Stories: British and American* (Boston: 1953), p. 43.

5. Naomi Lebowitz, "The Stories of J. F. Powers: The Sign of the Contradiction," *Kenyon Review,* XX (Summer, 1958), 499.

6. Scouffas, p. 50.

7. Carlos Villalobos Padilla, *The Art of Short Fiction in James Farl Powers* (Mexico City, 1963), p. 78.

8. E. Allison Peers, trans. & ed., *The Complete Works of Saint John of the Cross* (Westminster, Md., 1964), II, 29.

9. *Ibid.,* p. 140.

10. *Ibid.,* I, xxxv.

11. *Ibid.,* I, 386.

12. Padilla, p. 78.

13. Scouffas, p. 46.
14. Powers, letter to the author, July 11, 1962.
15. Alfred Kazin, "Gravity and Grace," *New Republic,* CXXII (April 30, 1956), 19-20.
16. Malloy, p. 75.
17. Robert O. Bowen, "Black Cat, White Collar," *Renascence,* IX (Autumn, 1956), 41.
18. Granville Hicks, "Living With Books," *New Leader,* XXXIX (March 26, 1956), 23.
19. Evelyn Waugh, "Scenes of Clerical Life," *Commonweal,* LXIII (March 30, 1956), 667.
20. Hence, it is not true that " 'Death of a Favorite' tells us nothing we do not already know about Father Burner" or that it "reads like an anecdotal footnote to 'Prince of Darkness' " (Sisk, p. 23). Nor is it quite true that Father Burner "is still a bully and a glutton" (John K. Hutchens, New York *Herald Tribune,* March 18, 1956, p. 2).
21. Winifred Lynskey, *Reading Modern Fiction* (3rd ed.; New York, 1962), p. 459.
22. Miss Lynskey's reading precedes that of Sylvan Barnet in *The Explicator,* XX (March, 1962), item 56.
23. Cleanth Brooks, John T. Purser, and R. P. Warren, *An Approach to Literature* (4th ed.; New York, 1964), p. 108.
24. I have revised the interpretation which I originally offered in *Insight I: Analyses of American Literature* (Frankfurt, Germany, 1962), pp. 220-25.
25. Powers, conversation with the author, November 30, 1964. Sweeney, the Monsignor's last name, has powerful negative connotations for readers who know the disgusting protagonist of T. S. Eliot's poems, "Sweeney Erect," "Sweeney Among the Nightingales," and "Sweeney Agonistes." The name also suggests "swine" or "whinny," both animal terms. And with his three initials. W. F. X., "the man could pass for a radio station" (127).
26. Robert Heilman, *Modern Short Stories* (New York, 1950), p. 337.
27. Some of Powers' critics welcomed this change. William Peden, for example, rejoiced that "his is the gentlest, most genial of satiric methods" ("The Tightrope Writers," *Virginia Quarterly Review,* XXXII [1956], 472). Others, like Leslie Fiedler, are disappointed that the jokes in *The Presence of Grace* have less of the diabolic than those in *Prince of Darkness* ("Some Footnotes on the Fiction of '56," *The Reporter,* XV [December 13, 1956], 46). Exactly why Powers' more benign humor, which laughs with rather than at his characters, should be considered an artistic decline is puzzling.
28. Hicks, p. 23.
29. Lebowitz, p. 498.
30. Kazin, *op. cit.*; O'Connor, "Reflection of a Petty World," *Saturday Review of Literature,* XXXIX (March 24, 1956), 22; Dorothy Van Ghent, *Yale Review,* ns XLV (Summer, 1956), 631; Donald Barr, New York *Times Book Review,* March 18, 1956, p. 5; Bowen, *op. cit.*; Hutchens, *op. cit.*; Sisk, *op. cit.*

31. Waugh. p. 668.
32. Sisk, p. 30.
33. John Raymond, review of *The Presence of Grace, New Statesman and Nation,* LII (September 29, 1956), 383.
34. Kazin, p. 20.
35. To some readers, like Leslie Fiedler, it appears that Powers here "tries the big subject . . . and cannot evoke the old authority of terror" (*op. cit.,* p. 46). But to others Powers in a small space clearly produces an immense drama in which the Devil has been reduced to a joker. As Myles comes to learn, in a straight game one must discard the joker. A more insightful critic, William Peden, has praised Powers' "remarkable sense of selectivity, his ability to isolate the significant from that which is merely interesting, his ability to select the inevitably right word, thought, gesture, or incident . . . his ability to suggest constantly the universal in the specific without recourse to the didactic or the ponderously symbolic" (*The American Short Story* [Boston, 1965]), pp. 79-80.
36. Cf. *Morte D'Urban,* p. 51 and Chapter 10.
37. John J. Kirvan, C.S.P., "Ostergothenburg Revisited," *The Catholic World,* CXCVIII (February, 1964), 308-9.
38. For example, the title itself (which, incidentally, picks up a metaphor from Powers' first great story, ('Lions, Harts, Leaping Does," in which it is said of Father Didymus that '(the keystone of his good intentions crumbled").
39. This central symbolism is reinforced by a number of smaller details—e.g., the fact that the Bishop subscribes to the Minneapolis *Tribune* (the distant standard of judgment), while Father Gau seeks the support of the local Ostergothenburg *Times.*
40. Cf. Powers, "Art, the Moon Prince."
41. Quoted by Philip Stratford, *Faith and Fiction* (Notre Dame, Ind., 1964), p. 23.
42. Sister Mary-Alice, O.P., "My Mentor, Flannery O'Connor," *Saturday Review,* XLVIII (May 29, 1965), 24.
43. Sisk, p. 35.
44. *Ibid,* p 38.
45. Bowen, pp. 40-41.
46. Van Ghent, pp. 630-31.

Chapter Four

1. McDonald, p. 21.
2. Page references parenthetically cited in the text are to *Morte D'Urban* (New York, 1962).
3. Saul Bellow, "Some Notes on Recent American Fiction," *Encounter,* XIX (November, 1963), 24.
4. F. W. Dupee, "In the Powers Country," *Partisan Review,* XXX (Spring, 1963), 115.
5. Klausler, "Sorrows of the Clementine," *The Christian Century,* LXXIX (November 14, 1962), 1390.
6. "Torments of a Good Man," *Time,* October 5, 1962, p. 62.

7. Phoebe Adams, "Reader's Choice," *Atlantic Monthly*, CCX (November, 1962), 134.

8. Thomas Curley, "J. F. Powers' Long-Awaited First Novel," *Commonweal*, LXXVII (October 12, 1962), 77.

9. Harvey Curtis Webster, "Comedy and Darkness," *Kenyon Review*, XXV (1963), 167-68.

10. William H. Gass, "Bingo Game at the Foot of the Cross," *The Nation*, CXCV (September 29, 1962), 183.

11. Granville Hicks, "The Foibles of Good Men," *Saturday Review* XLV (September 15, 1962), 21.

12. Martin Price, review of *Morte D'Urban, Yale Review*, ns LII (December, 1962), 263.

13. John P. Sisk, review of *Morte D'Urban, Renascence*, XVI (1963), 101.

14. P. Hinchcliffe, "Nightmare of Grace," *Blackfriars*, XLV (February, 1964), 61-69; Marie J. Henault, "The Saving of Father Urban," *America*, CVIII (March 2, 1963), 290-92.

15. *Ibid.*, p. 292.

16. Powers' source for the epigraph from James M. Barrie's *The Little Minister* (1891) was the autobiography of Walter Hagen, the golfer. Father Urban says, "[Hagen] was raised in the Church, you know" (196).

17. Leo J. Hertzel, among others, suggests that *Morte D'Urban* is a *roman à clef*: "members of the Order of Friars Minor, particularly those of the large midwestern province, believe that Powers draws extensively on his early contacts with their Order. . . . The fumbling, sometimes lurching policies and practices of the Order of St. Clement . . . bear such a close resemblance to some of the happenings in Franciscan provinces that it is difficult to suppose that the order which appears in the book bears no relationship to Franciscan reality. (Readers who enjoy this sort of game could perhaps identify the persons and places included in the first part of Chapter Four of *Morte D'Urban*)." *Renascence*, XVIII (1965), 208-9.

In a reply to a direct question about this matter, Powers said, "Msgr M is drawn from the late Msgr Formaz, Our Saviour's Church, Jacksonville [Illinois], who baptized me and on whom I called in 1957 (I think it was) which was our next meeting (after my baptism, I mean, in 1917). He was a tiny man, Swiss parentage, a wit and bon viveur, pince nez, frock coat, fond of the old Lafayette Hotel in New York, in love (for some reason) with St. Louis (Mo.). . . . He was a legendary figure in the Springfield diocese, and died a few years ago, still in charge, above the ruck of small town life. . . . Father Placidus is my own creation, but perhaps Father Bernardine had something to do with it: I still admire him, Big Ben, but at a distance. I still recall the pleasure I received once when, at a football game, I made a shoestring tackle, bringing down the runner who would've been in the clear but for that, and heard Fr Bernardine's voice come out of the crowd after the play, 'Attaboy, Jimmy.'" Letter to the author, July 16, 1965.

Father Edgar Eberle, O.F.M., one of Powers' teachers at the Quincy

Academy, writes that "Fr. Placidus' physical size, his love for sports, his interest in the athletic program of the school remind me of Fr. Bernardine Teppe, O.F.M. He was in charge of the high school section during Powers' freshman year at the Academy. He was something of a legend at Quincy. The boys called him "Big Ben." He was about six feet four or five inches tall and quite heavy. He loved to don a big baseball suit and do fungo batting for the boys. He was usually on hand for football and baseball practices, as well as for the games. . . . In the classroom he was an excellent teacher of Latin and Greek—quite demanding. But after class he could chat with groups of boys, razz them about their teams, their local ball clubs. . . . [However], in my opinion the characters of Msgr. Morez and Fr. Placidus are fictitious. I cannot identify them with priests who taught at Quincy Academy." Letter to the author, June 20, 1965.

18. Powers has cited Msgr. Renton as one of the moral norms of the novel. Cf. Malloy, p. 75.

19. Hayden Carruth, "Reviving the Age of Satire," *The New Republic*, CXLVII (September 24, 1962), 24.

20. Price, p. 263.

21. Bellow, p. 24.

22. Collignon, "Powers' *Morte D'Urban*: A Layman's Indictment," *Renascence*, XVI (1963), 21.

23. Powers had once commented on F. Scott Fitzgerald's use of this theme: "One story he wrote on a conceivably Catholic subject, 'Absolution,' is good enough. Its priest could be as authentic as any one of a hundred different kinds of priest, but it is significant that this particular one had quite a feeling for blonde girls . . . and had a ceaseless hankering for the other life, meaning pop corn and peanuts and ferris wheels, which for a priest in the Dakotas, trust Fitzgerald, comes to about the same thing as the author getting his in New York and Paris." "Dealer in Diamonds and Rhinestones," p. 410.

24. Dupee, p. 115.

25. No doubt the source for this (as my graduate assistant, Lesley Brill, points out) is the wood-cut of a stylized stag, entitled "Live-Waters," which accompanied Powers' first publication, "A Day in the County Jail."

26. It is also reminiscent of John Donne's assertion that "certainly he that loves not the Militant Church, hath but a faint faith in his interest in the Triumphant. He that cares not though the materiall Church fall, I am afraid is falling from the spirituall." *L Sermons*, 36: 330.

27. As, indeed, it does. It is a reference to the "Joyus Isle surrounded by broad water where Lancelot (the greatest name of any knight) assumed the title of the knight who has trespassed and lived with Lady Elaine." Hinchcliffe, p. 66.

28. Sisk, p. 103.

29. Lucy Johnson, "Peanut Eating Pull," *Progressive*, XXVI (October, 1962), 50.

30. James G. Murray, review of *Morte D'Urban*, *The Critic*, XXI (October-November, 1962), 84. Murray errs—the motto of the Order is "We go where the Lord Willeth," as Hinchcliffe points out, p. 64.

31. Hyman, "The Priest with the Fish-Net Hatband," *The New Leader,* XLV (September 17, 1962), 23.

32. Adams, p. 135.

33. Kirvan, p. 308.

34. Thomas Merton, "*Morte D'Urban*: Two Celebrations," *Worship,* XXXVI (November, 1962), 645.

35. Curley, p. 78.

36. Henault, p. 290. Miss Henault adds in a letter to the author, December 2, 1964: "Powers used, I believe, the boys' Arthur book (Howard Pyle?) or his memories of it more than Malory, to whom he probably turned only after his imagination had done the major part of the work." This, too, is very astute, for Powers has said that "as a boy, my favorite authors were James Willard Schultz, Ralph Henry Barbour, and Howard Pyle," Hoehn, II, 455. And in the autobiographical story, "Jamesie," we read that the boy had on his shelf "Sir Lancelot, Merlin, Sir Tristram, King Arthur. . . . But they turned out wrong, most of them, with all the good guys dying or turning into fairies, and the bad guys becoming dwarfs."

Also interesting in the light of Powers' professed admiration for Sinclair Lewis is Lewis' comment that "the only source for *Main Street* that I am aware of was Malory's *Morte D'Arthur*; I wrote *Main Street* because there was nothing like Malory in the Middle West." Theodore Spencer, "The Critic's Function," *Sewanee Review,* XLVII (1939), 556.

37. Dupee, p. 115.

38. Malloy, p. 80.

39. Powers denies any symbolic significance to the name of Dr. Fish and says that on second thought "Dr. Jass" would have been a better name. Conversation with the author, November 30, 1964.

40. Malloy, p. 76.

41. *Ibid.*

42. G. B. Caird, *The Gospel of St. Luke* (Pelican Books, 1963), p. 185. Powers has used the Luke motif throughout his work beginning with "Prince of Darkness." There is an interesting similarity between his preoccupation with the parable and that of Robert Lowell, who in "The Children of Light" (*Land of Unlikeness,* 1944) interprets the parable as "expressing regret that the children of light cannot store for heaven with the same sagacity as the children of earth store for this world." Neville Braybrooke, "Robert Lowell and the Unjust Steward," *Dalhousie Review,* XLIV (Spring, 1964), 30. Interesting also is Joyce's use of the parable, in a way similar to Powers', in the closing section of "Grace" in *Dubliners.*

43. Malloy, p. 76.

44. *Ibid.,* p. 80.

45. Hicks, p. 21.

46. Curley, p. 77.

47. F. J. Gallagher, review of *Morte D'Urban, America,* CVII (November 24, 1962), 1139.

48. E. P. J. Corbett, review of *Morte D'Urban, America,* CVII (September 15, 1962), 737.

49. Adams, p. 134.

50. Richard Sullivan, "Babbitt in Cassock," New York *Times Book Review*, September 16, 1962, pp. 4-5.

51. Patrick J. O'Halloran, S.J., review of *Morte D'Urban, Review of Religion*, XXII (May, 1963), 371.

52. Kleber Haedens, review of *Morte D'Urban, Nouveau Candide*, Dec. 5, 1963; and Michel Mohrt, "Une prêtre américaine," *Le Monde*, Dec. 7, 1963.

53. Murray, p. 84.

54. Carruth, p. 24.

55. Merton, pp. 645-46.

56. A study of the clerical reviews of *Morte D'Urban* reveals more about the clergy than about the novel—and confirms Powers' portrayal of priests who would rather pull rank than face criticism. This is especially true of reviews written by Irish priests in what Powers has described as "the juicy Hibernian tone" (Malloy, p. 66). For example, Thomas Rowan, C.S.S.R., said: "A priest reader of this stuff is liable to feel the urge to send the author a diocesan directory with a check-list of sound citizens among the clergy worthwhile meeting. . . . His sense of humor is bound to lose a lot of its muscle-tone after being subjected to so much of what Saintsbury, referring to Augustine satire, called 'superfluous nastiness.'" "*Morte D'Urban*: A Novel About Priests," *Homiletic and Pastoral Review*, LXIII (1963), 291-94.

In a similar vein, Msgr. John S. Kennedy wrote, "I must say that the emphasis in this book strikes me as unbalanced and intrinsically false. It is almost entirely negative. The positive—in priestly spirit, sacrifice, endurance, accomplishment—is wholly missing from the picture. But in reality they are there and operative. Hence the picture is a narrowly squinting and selective version of reality, and woefully misleading." *Our Sunday Visitor*, September 2, 1963.

57. Herbert McArthur, "Tragic and Comic Modes," *Criticism*, III (Winter, 1961), 36-45.

58. Malloy, pp. 73-74.

59. Though Powers claims to be unfamiliar with Dante, the action of *Morte D'Urban* can be seen as a movement from Inferno through Purgatorio to Paradiso. Even Urban's two dunkings parallel Dante's two immersions in water at the approaches to Paradiso.

60. Marie Collins Swabey, *Comic Laughter* (New Haven, 1961), pp. 240-41.

Selected Bibliography

PRIMARY SOURCES

Individual stories are listed in order of prior publication below the volume in which they are collected.

1. *Books: Novel and Collected Stories*

Prince of Darkness and other stories. Garden City, N.Y.: Doubleday & Co., 1947. British edition: John Lehmann, 1948. Paperback: Doubleday Image Book, 1958.

"He Don't Plant Cotton," *Accent,* III (Winter, 1943), 106-13.

"Lions, Harts, Leaping Does," *Accent*, IV (Autumn, 1943), 12-29.

"Renner," *New Mexico Quarterly Review*, XIV (Spring, 1944), 37-46.

"The Trouble," *Commonweal*, XLI (November 10, 1944), 97-101.

"The Old Bird, A Love Story," *Rocky Mountain Review*, IX (Fall, 1944), 5-13.

"Prince of Darkness," *Accent*, VI (Winter, 1946), 79-107.

"The Valiant Woman," *Accent*, VII (Spring, 1947), 150-56.

"Jamesie," a revised version of "Baseball Bill," *Colliers*, CXIX (April 26, 1947), 102-13 *passim.*

"The Eye." No prior publication.

"The Forks." No prior publication.

"The Lord's Day," in *Cross-Section 1947*, edited by E. Seaver. New York: 1947, pp. 13-19.

The Presence of Grace. Garden City, N.Y.: Doubleday & Co., 1956. British edition: Gollancz, 1956. Paperback: Atheneum, 1962.

"The Poor Thing," a revised version of "Teresa," *Tomorrow*, IX (October, 1949), 35-39.

"Death of a Favorite," *The New Yorker*, XXVI (July 1, 1950), 23-30.

"Defection of a Favorite," *The New Yorker*, XXVII (November 10, 1951), 35-42.

"The Devil Was the Joker," *The New Yorker*, XXIX (March 21, 1953), 36-59 *passim.*

"The Presence of Grace," *Accent*, XIII (Autumn, 1953), 195-215; also published in *The London Magazine*, II (May, 1955), 32-51.

"Blue Island," *Accent*, XV (Autumn, 1955), 243-54.

"A Losing Game," *The New Yorker*, XXXI (November 5, 1955), 44-48.

"Dawn," *Partisan Review*, XXIII (Winter, 1956), 13-22.

"Zeal," *Commonweal*, LIII (February 10, 1956), 487-92.

Morte D'Urban. Garden City, N.Y.: Doubleday & Co., 1962. British edition: Gollancz, 1962. Paperback: Popular Library, 1963. Reprint: Modern Library, 1967.

"The Green Banana," *The New Yorker*, XXXII (November 10, 1956), 48-58.

"A Couple of Nights Before Christmas," *The New Yorker*, XXXIII (December 21, 1957), 28-36, 38.
"Wrens and Starlings," *The New Yorker*, XXXVI (May 21, 1960), 39-48.
"God Writes a Bad Hand," *The New Yorker*, XXXVI (October 15, 1960), 44-50.
"Sailing Against the Wind," *The Kenyon Review*, XXIV (Spring, 1962), 257-80.
"The Most a Man Can Do," *The Critic*, XX (March, 1962), 41.
"Twenty-Four Hours in a Strange Diocese," *Esquire*, LVII (April, 1962), 66.
"At Lake Lucille," *The Critic*, XX (July, 1962), 17-19.

2. *Uncollected Stories and Sketches*

"Night in the County Jail," *Catholic Worker*, X (May, 1943), 8.
"Day in the County Jail," *Catholic Worker*, X (July, 1943), 6-7.
"Saint on the Air," *Catholic Worker*, X (December, 1943), 8.
"Interlude in a Book Shop," *Opportunity*, XXII (Winter, 1944), 22-24.
"Blessing," *The Sign*, XXV (August, 1945), 18-20.
"Look How the Fish Live," *The Reporter*, XVII (October 31, 1957), 36-42.
"Keystone," *The New Yorker*, XXXIX (May 18, 1963), 42-46, 48, 50, 53, 56, 59-60, 62, 65-67, 70, 72, 75-76, 78, 81.

3. *Occasional Writings: Articles, Satires, Reviews*

"William Everson: *War Elegies* and *Waldport Poems*" (Review), *Accent*, V (Spring, 1945), 190-91.
"William Maxwell: *The Folded Leaf*, and Walter Van Tilburg Clark: *The City of Trembling Leaves*," (Reviews), *Accent*, V (Summer, 1945), 244-46.
"Dealer in Diamonds and Rhinestones" (Review of F. Scott Fitzgerald: *The Crack-Up*), *Commonweal*, XLII (August 10, 1945), 408-10.
"Peter Taylor: *A Long Fourth and Other Stories*" (Review), *Commonweal*, XLVIII (June 25, 1948), 262-63.
"Waugh Out West" (Review of Evelyn Waugh's *The Loved One*), *Commonweal*, XLVIII (July 16, 1948), 326-27.
"Fun With a Purpose," *Commonweal*, XLIX (October 15, 1948), 9-12.
"Refugee" (Review of Sean O'Faolain: *The Short Story*), *The Month* (London), ns I (May, 1949), 336-38.
"St. Paul, Home of the Saints," *Partisan Review*, XVI (July, 1949), 714-21.
"Short and Select" (Review of Msgr. Ronald Knox: *The Occasional Sermons*), *Commonweal*, L (August 5, 1949), 415-17.
"Peddling Fish" (Review of F. O. Tremaine: *Short Story Writing*), *Commonweal*, LI (November 4, 1949), 122-28.
"Elizabeth Bowen *et al.*, *Why Do I Write?*" (Review), *Renascence*, II (Spring, 1950), 169.
Letter to the Editor, Brooklyn *Tablet*, August 19, 1950, p. 6.
Letter to the Editor, *Books on Trial*, XV (November, 1956), 110.
"Are These Our Children?," *The Nation*, CXC (December 10, 1960), 453-54.

"Moonshot," *The Nation*, CXCII (March 3, 1962), 195-96, 204.

"Cross-Section: Authors in Wonderland" (Reply to questionnaire), *The Critic*, XXI (October-November, 1962), 67.

"She Stands Alone" (Commentary on Katherine Anne Porter), *Four Quarters*, XII (November, 1962), 56.

". . . of the Author as a Responsible Storyteller" (National Book Award Address), *New York Times Book Review*, May 12, 1963, p. 2.

"The Pesky Side of Paradise" (Review of Daniel Callahan, ed.: *Generation of the Third Eye* and Edward M. Keating: *The Scandal of Silence*), *New York Herald Tribune Book Review*, May 23, 1965, pp. 5, 16.

"Conscience and Religion" (Review of Gordon Zahn: *In Solitary Witness*), *Commentary*, XL (July, 1965), 91-92.

SECONDARY SOURCES

I. *Bibliographies*

PADILLA, [BROTHER] CARLOS VILLALOBOS [F.M.S.]. *The Art of Short Fiction in J. F. Powers*. Universidad Autonoma de Mexico, 1963. Pp. 114-19 of a full-length study of Powers' short stories.

WEDGE, GEORGE F. "J. F. Powers," *Critique*, II (1958), 63-70.

II. *Biographical Data (exclusive of those in standard biographical references)*

HAMILL, PETE. "The Art of J. F. Powers," *New York Post Sunday Magazine*, March 24, 1963, p. 10. An account of a candid interview on the occasion of the National Book Award.

HUTCHINSON, TOM. "Talk with J. F. Powers," *Catholic Messenger*, April 16, 1959, p. 2. Reprinted in *The Critic*, XVI (June-July, 1959), 50. In which Powers discusses his writing habits and his faith and the sad state of Catholic journals.

LUNDEGAARD, BOB. "Author: 'Writing is Sweaty Job,'" *Minneapolis Sunday Tribune*, April 7, 1963, Feature Section, pp. 1, 6. A home-town view of the writer, including an interview in which Powers asserts his social and religious convictions.

MALLOY, SISTER M. KRISTIN, O.S.B. "The Catholic and Creativity: J. F. Powers," *American Benedictine Review*, XV (March, 1964), 63-80. The single most valuable source of Powers' own view of his background, his social and literary milieu, and his fiction.

MCDONALD, DONALD. "Interview with J. F. Powers," *The Critic*, XIX (October-November, 1960), 20-21, 88-90. Reprinted in *Catholics in Conversation*, New York: 1960. Powers' account of the themes and techniques of his earlier stories and a description of *Morte D'Urban* as a work in progress.

III. *Selected List of Studies and Reviews*

Only a few of the many citations in the "Notes and References" are listed here.

COGLEY, JOHN. Review of *Prince of Darkness*, *Catholic Worker*, XIV (July-August, 1947), 5. A comparison of Powers and Harry Sylvester, two writers who deal with "the spiritual anemia found among the parochial clergy," with some excellent early insights into the difference between slick cynicism and compassionate satire.

HENAULT, MARIE. "The Saving of Father Urban," *America*, CVIII (March 2, 1963), 290-92. A brilliant discussion of the Arthurian motifs in *Morte D'Urban.*

HINCHLIFFE, ARNOLD P. "Nightmare of Grace," *Blackfriars*, XLV (February, 1964), 61-69. A very fine treatment of the "Mammon of Iniquity" theme in *Morte D'Urban.*

LEBOWITZ, NAOMI. "The Stories of J. F. Powers: The Sign of the Contradiction," *Kenyon Review*, XX (Summer, 1958), 494-99. A study of the "dialectical tension involving secularism and divinity" in the clerical stories.

MERTON, THOMAS. "*Morte D'Urban*: Two Celebrations," *Worship*, XXXVI (November, 1962), 645-50. The great monk and priest defends Powers against charges of anticlericalism and describes *Morte D'Urban* as a "work of literary genius . . . that makes a specifically religious statement."

QUINN, SISTER M. BERNETTA, O.S.F. "View from a Rock: The Fiction of Flannery O'Connor and J. F. Powers," *Critique*, II (Fall, 1958), 19-27. A comparison which concludes with the judgment that "there is a difference, in Miss O'Connor's favor, in the depths to which they see" the spiritual life.

SCOUFFAS, GEORGE. "J. F. Powers: On the Vitality of Disorder," *Critique*, II (Fall, 1958), 41-58. A careful study which, though it errs in concluding that "in no story of Powers is there an ultimate resolution," elucidates a typical "centripetal movement . . . [which] slowly whirls toward a still point of revelation that in a sense negates all hierarchies."

SISK, JOHN P. "The Complex Moral Vision of J. F. Powers," *Critique*, II (Fall, 1958), 28-40. Finds it "important for American literature" that Powers' fiction "intellectualizes itself without losing its direct approach." This article and Sisk's review of *Morte D'Urban* in *Renascence* (1963) constitute one of the important discussions of J. F. Powers.

Index

Index